P9-CDF-078

A New Kind of Church

A Systems Approach

By Dan R. Dick with Evelyn Burry

DISCIPLESHIP
RESOURCES

PO BOX 340003, NASHVILLE TN, 37203-0003
www.discipleshipresources.org

Reprinted 2000, 2006

Cover design by Shawn Lancaster
Book design by Joey McNair

ISBN 0-88177-484-7 (10)
Library of Congress Control Number 2006928690

Table of Contents

Foreword

The word "new" does not always mean "never seen before." It can also mean "unfamiliar," "fresh," or "revitalized." It is this spirit that this book — first written almost a decade ago — hopes to capture. We need a new kind of church. Ironically, the way to learn to be new is to look to our heritage and history. Everything we need to know to create a vibrant, vital, transformative church exists in our past.

Our age is one of enormous spiritual hunger, an insatiable quest for meaning and purpose, and an incredible desire to make a difference in the world. This is true not only of church attending Christians, but people of many faiths, traditions, worldviews, and cultures. Coincidentally, ours is also an age of overwhelming amounts of data, information, opinion, spin, advertising, promotion, and persuasion. We are buffeted and beaten by the waves and currents of media messages that make it more confusing — rather than less — to make sense of our world. What an incredible opportunity for the church!

In 2006, I completed a study of spiritual seekers in North America who, for one reason or another, have no affiliation with a church or religious institution. The reasons they offer are many, but some of the most compelling are:
- The church is not a safe space to raise questions and explore doubts.
- The church seems more focused on keeping people out than welcoming them in.
- People active in church don't seem to know their own story — what they believe, why it's important, and what the symbols and rituals of their faith mean.
- They want to be challenged, supported, and assisted to align their articulated values — what they say is important — with their lived values — their actual day-to-day behaviors.
- They want a loving, affirming, and accepting environment where they can discover who God made them to be.

In other words, they need a kind of church that they have not been able to find — a church that cares more about the needs of the world than the needs of the congregation, that spends more money on others than on itself, that spends more time out in the world sharing the good news than it does gathered behind closed doors, and that provides a bright, shining example of love, justice, and mercy for an often cold and cruel world. They're looking for a new kind of church.

But so are long-time church members. Recent surveys reveal that many thirty-plus year members wish their church:
- Acted more, and talked about acting less
- Spent less money on facility & staff, and spent more on ministry to those in need

- Got back to the basics of prayer, Bible study, and Christian service (devoting less time to meetings, dinners, bazaars, coffee houses, etc.)
- Helped them apply their faith to daily life
- Talked more about God and God's will and less about human needs and desires
- Care as deeply about the faith needs of those in the church as they seem to be the needs of those we have yet to reach (as one person said, "It would be nice to come to worship for people who love God instead of a thinly-veiled attempt at evangelism for people who don't yet know God")

The time is right. People both inside and outside of the traditional mainline denominations want something different, relevant, and real — they want a new kind of church. By God's grace, Jesus' example, and the guidance of the Holy Spirit, may we become such a church.

Dan Dick, 2006

Introduction

"Is there a future for The United Methodist Church? This question is raised throughout the denomination. The answers range from a stark pessimism to unbridled optimism. Some feel that all differences will be reconciled and that the "united" in United Methodism will prevail. Others go so far as to predict an imminent split in the denomination. Only time will tell which forecast is true.

A NEW KIND OF CHURCH offers perspective on this debate, and explores some of the critical issues that may help shape our future. It is not a "prescription" for fixing the church, but a clarion call to objectively assess the current state of the church and make some important decisions as we plan for the future.

A NEW KIND OF CHURCH requires a new kind of thinking. Borrowing concepts from systems theory, complexity theory, and developmental theory, a theory of church emerges — a way of responding to the fast-paced change of our post-modern world. A careful reexamination of what we do, why we do it, and what we believe will be the result of all our faithful efforts is central to this book.

A NEW KIND OF CHURCH is a workbook for congregational leaders — laity and clergy together — striving to be effective in our time of monumental change. The type of transformation called for requires dynamic spiritual leadership, faithfully pursuing God's will and vision for the church. The necessary changes in the church will not happen naturally — they require courage, commitment, and the desire for something better. We cannot achieve a new and vital church by continuing to do the same old things the same old way. Our leaders must be willing to try new things in new ways, taking some risks, and embracing the prophetic role of change-agents.

The book is divided into three sections, with questions for discussion and reflection at the end of each chapter.

The first section, titled "Where Have We Been?", examines the historical journey from the New Testament to the present day. Chapter One, "A People of God," looks at the models of the church presented by Jesus and Paul. It answers the question, "What does it mean to be a people of God?" Chapter Two examines "Our Wesleyan Heritage" by looking at the vision of the church presented by John Wesley. Chapter Three, "To the Present Day," explores the evolution of The United Methodist Church in the twentieth century.

Section Two deals with the question "Where Are We Now?" Four chapters deal with The United Methodist Church in relationship to the world at the end of the twentieth century. Chapter Four identifies "Where We Are in Time"; Chapter Five locates "Where We Are in the World"; Chapter Six examines "Where We Are as a Society"; and Chapter Seven names "Where We Are as Spiritual Seekers."

The third section gazes into the future to ask, "Where Are We Heading?" Chapters Eight through Eleven cast a vision for The United Methodist Church into the early twenty-first century and examine the critical issues for designing a strong church structure. Chapter Eight defines "Systems and Process Thinking" as a better way to understand the church. Chapter Nine describes the understanding of "Core Values, Mission, and Vision" as the way to lay a firm foundation for building new systems for ministry. Chapter Ten examines the role of leadership in "Learning Leaders." Chapter Eleven, "Breaking Free," challenges the leaders of The United Methodist Church, both lay and clergy, to interrupt the inertia that holds the church to its current trajectory and to develop a new course for the future.

A NEW KIND OF CHURCH is intended as a book of hope. Many books decry the sorry state of The United Methodist Church, but there is much more reason to rejoice than to despair. God continues to bless us with a gospel of grace and light and life. Our congregations are full to overflowing with spiritual gifts, talents, knowledge, experience, and ability. We own incredible buildings and properties, manage resources, and have much to share with each other and with the world. In every place, at every time, God provides us with untold opportunities to love, to serve, to care, and to heal. As God makes new every day the glories of creation, so, too, we as God's people may make new our life together as the body of Christ — becoming a new kind of church for a new age.

Section 1

Where Have We Been?

Chapter One:
A People of God

If Jesus Christ walked into a United Methodist Church, would he recognize it as a product of the movement he set in motion twenty centuries ago? Would he be pleased or distressed by what he sees? Would it cause him to settle in or to depart quickly? How would Jesus respond to an experience of The United Methodist Church in North America?

These are simple, but compelling questions. To answer them, we need some perspective on the church that Jesus initiated and how it compares with the church today. The lists below present some key characteristics of the church that Jesus created and the way it evolved under the leadership of the Apostle Paul. The Pauline model most closely resembles The United Methodist Church that exists today.

Jesus	Paul
Focus on people, community, building relationships	Focus on organizational design for ministry
Mobile, the church goes to the people	Stationary, people come to the church
Preaching, teaching, and healing performed as needed, every day of the week	Preaching, teaching primarily on Sunday; healing primarily the work of the ordained clergy
Frequent breaks with tradition	Bound by tradition
Grace-based, means are as important as ends	Rule-based, the ends justify the means

Jesus	Paul
Highly inclusive	Struggling to be inclusive
Teacher-disciple model	Shepherd-flock model
Focus on relationship with God	Focus on relationship with the local congregation

Many more contrasts emerge from a survey of Scripture alongside the reality of The United Methodist Church. The comparisons are not meant to chastise the church. Not one characteristic of the current reality of the church is necessarily negative. Each quality of Paul's model (listed on the right) was designed to help support the vision of Jesus Christ (as defined by the list on the left). With time, however, many structures and practices of the church took the central focus away from the things they were designed to ensure.

Jesus never let his focus stray from people. Whether these people were disciples, the crowds, or his enemies, Jesus turned his full attention to his relationships with them. Jesus summarized the entire content of the law as "'You shall love the Lord your God with all your heart, and with all your soul, and with all your mind.' This is the greatest and first commandment. And a second is like it: 'You shall love your neighbor as yourself'" (Matthew 22:37-39, NRSV). Jesus never indicated *how* this was to be done (structure), just that it *must* be done (mission). Throughout history, leaders of the church have designed organizational structures to facilitate the love of God and neighbor. The current organizational design of The United Methodist Church was created to guarantee this focus.

When the focus of the church is on people, the church goes where the people are, not the other way around. The church of Jesus Christ and the twelve disciples was a mobile church. It was not in a fixed location; instead, it existed in the cities and towns, in the country, on the roadways, and by the seaside. The church catered to the affluent and the poor, the educated and the simple, and the religious and the secular. No one was excluded from the ministry of the church, because the church went everywhere. In our day, churches spread their influence far and wide by sheer numbers of locations; but because they are property-bound, they invite people to come to them rather than canvassing the community. Although many churches do extend their ministries beyond the parameters of their physical location, most churches are seen as "locations" more readily than as "mobile ministry units."

Just as today's church is location-bound, it is also time-bound. Churches establish "hours of operation." Worship services and educational opportunities are offered on specific days at specific times. The model that Jesus provided was a "just-in-time" church, where preaching, teaching, and healing were offered whenever they were needed. "Church" was not what happened on Sunday morning at 11:00. Church was people in ministry to people all the time. Jesus was not the only person to preach, teach, and heal. The disciples were partners in ministry. It was never Jesus' "job" to spread the good news; it was the mission of the entire group.

This flexibility of meeting people where they were, whenever they had need, created problems for Jesus — when he broke the Sabbath, for example. Repeatedly, Jesus violated the sacred tradition of the Jewish faith to care for people. Traditions, rituals, and practices should serve the mission of bringing people to God. If they didn't serve that purpose, Jesus disregarded them. The United Methodist Church has established many traditions, practices, and policies that hold us in place and often prevent us from serving the needs of people. Whereas Jesus moved the church from law to grace, today we temper grace with the law of the denomination.

The model of interaction that Jesus used was that of teacher-disciple. Jesus trained the disciples for ministry by instructing, modeling, and mentoring. He worked closely with his students to mold them into ministers of the gospel. Each trainee had a name and a face, and Jesus kept the size of the group manageable so that he could deal personally with the individuals. Over time, as the church gained popularity and greater numbers, the teacher-disciple model gave way to the shepherd-flock model. This is the model most prevalent today. In it, a pastor (shepherd) tends a large group of people, giving general guidance and instruction. Most teaching in this model is of a universal nature that does not always speak to the particular realities of individuals. Due to the size of today's congregations, personal attention is limited. The nurture of individuals' gifts and abilities gives way to group settings. Mentoring is limited, and — in cases where the ordained pastor serves as the single leader of the congregation — may not occur at all. Training has evolved from a personal, custom-tailored process to a variety of classes, seminars, programs, and workshops.

The shepherd-flock model is more hierarchical than the teacher-disciple model. In the shepherd-flock model, the pastor serves as a chief executive officer of the organization. In the teacher-disciple model, the pastor serves as a "first among equals," where the purpose is to develop autonomous teachers who can instruct a whole new level of disciples. The shepherd-flock model has an "us-them" component built in that separates the clergy from the laity.

The design of Jesus Christ is much more inclusive than the existent model in The United Methodist Church. Jesus, and later Paul, moved beyond the distinctions of male, female; Jew, Gentile; slave, free; rich, poor; and so on to include everyone in the grace of God. Anyone could serve God, anyone could be in ministry, and no one was excluded from receiving ministry. When the disciples complained that those of lesser reputation were teaching and healing, Jesus calmed them by saying that it didn't matter who did the work of God as long as the work got done.

The modern church places great emphasis on meeting certain criteria, performing certain tasks, and achieving certain standards before allowing people to serve Christ. Elaborate processes determine who will lead and how they will lead: clergy have an ordination process; laity leaders have training programs. Jesus opened the ranks to thieves, sorcerers, prostitutes, and the formerly demon-possessed. The debate over whether to include women, certain ethnic groups, other cultures, other faith traditions, and those choosing alternative lifestyles has, at times, been divisive and devastating in The United Methodist Church. These struggles are not over yet, but Jesus' inclusive modeling as shown in Scripture offers guidance.

Jesus' ultimate focus was on people's relationship with God. For Jesus, all structures, practices, rituals, and beliefs must serve to bring people closer to God. Whatever did not strengthen this relationship, Jesus disregarded.

The reality today is that we emphasize the relationship to the church as much as we emphasize the relationship to God. The amount of time, energy, money, and resources that we channel into the maintenance of structure, facilities, programs, and staff only marginally support the focus of helping people develop a strong relationship with God and neighbor. When our structures for ministry get in the way of the very ministries they were designed to ensure, it is time for change.

Jesus created a new kind of church. The challenge for The United Methodist Church is to develop a structure that is appropriate to the needs and demands of the contemporary culture and that is grounded in the vision that Jesus revealed. This church will focus on people and their relationships with God. It will create communities of believers, sharing a sense of call and pursuing a vision for ministry grounded in the values of the people. The church will be a faithful steward of its gifts and resources, the communities in which it serves, the larger society and the planet, and the future. The church will be inclusive, not only of those people it deems acceptable, but also of those who challenge its sensibilities. It will recapture its commitment to honor and glorify God in all that it says and does.

Chapter One Questions

1. What might a congregation that integrates the "Jesus" and "Paul" models of the church look like?

2. What would be some of the benefits of such integration?

3. What are the potential obstacles or challenges to integrating the two models?

4. The word "new" is used in this context as "unfamiliar" or "different." In what ways is a congregation that integrates the two models "new?" What would be new for your congregation? What would be familiar?

Chapter Two:
Our Wesleyan Heritage

I n the middle of the eighteenth century, John Wesley recognized that the Church of England had lost its focus on helping people build relationships with God. The church existed as a fortress, isolated from the problems and pressures of the society. The Anglican Church cared more for its own survival than for the salvation of the people. Wesley saw the masses of people who never attended church and wondered who attended to their spiritual needs. Violating the conventions of the church, Wesley traveled to the piers, pubs, and street corners to proclaim the saving love of Jesus Christ. Wesley received severe criticism for his lack of institutional concern and his break from established tradition.

John Wesley realized that the Church of England had displaced Christian community with institutional structure. Methodism emerged from his concern for the integrity of the church. Maintaining the institution of the church was important, but only as long as the institution fulfilled the fundamental mission of the church.

Wesley felt that the primary message of the church should be God's grace. Prevenient grace prepares the way for reconciliation with God; justifying grace brings people back into right relationship with God through the sacrifice of Christ; and sanctifying grace empowers people to remain faithful to their covenantal connection with God. Although God's grace cannot be earned by human action, Wesley taught that there were significant practices that put men and women squarely in the path of that grace. Practicing the means of grace opened people to experience God's love in a real way. The church was the place where people joined together in community to practice the means of grace and support one another in the faith.

The list of the means of grace varies in the writings of John Wesley, but they include prayer, the study of Scripture, attendance at the Lord's Supper, fasting, Christian conference, and acts of mercy. Every list where Wesley speaks of the means of grace contains prayer, the study of Scripture, and attendance at the Lord's Supper. Fasting, or abstinence, referred to moderation and self-control of earthly passions. Christian conference referred to the special conversation of Christians where they shared their faith and held one another accountable in spiritual discipline and the practice of the other means of grace. Acts of mercy represent acts of kindness, compassion, giving, and sharing to care for others. The practice of the means of grace, Wesley believed, gave Christians their identity. Practicing the means of grace set people apart from the rest of society. The Church of England in the early 1700s had strayed from the communal practice of the means of grace; and in Wesley's estimation, the church had lost its identity as a faithful people of God. The earliest Methodist societies, classes, and bands were established around the practice of the means of grace.

Early Methodism also reclaimed some of the best qualities of the Jesus model of the church. It was mobile (itinerant), and its focus was on helping people build relationships with God and neighbor. Because the church depended upon traveling preachers, Methodist services were held whenever the people could gather together. It offered both regular Sunday services and weekly worship, education, and fellowship opportunities. Since the ordained clergy were absent more often than they were present, the ongoing ministry of the church in each community depended on the laity. Ordinary men and women were the leaders and teachers of the early class meetings. Almost everything about the early Methodist Church was a break from Anglican tradition, especially as it emerged in America.

Very quickly, the church became highly structured, and the continuously evolving *Book of Discipline* ordered its doctrine and polity. Churches were "planted," and pastors were "appointed." Fewer weekday church experiences were offered; and with the creation of the Sunday school, the church became the place people gathered, rather than the designation of who the people were. The concepts of "mission" and "evangelism" became less about our identity and purpose as they became programs of the congregation. People gave money and sent missionaries instead of engaging in direct service, and evangelism devolved from sharing the gospel to inviting people to church. The inclusiveness that characterized the fledgling Methodist movement gave way to segregation and gender politics. Wesley's vision of the church being a servant to the world gave way to a lesser vision of the people in service to the institution.

At various points in the history of The United Methodist Church, the pendulum swung back the other way. Whenever the structure of the church has precluded building strong relationships with God and neighbor, there has been a movement back toward our roots. Small groups, alternative worship styles, greater inclusiveness and celebration of diversity, the resurgence of the laity in leadership, and a deep spiritual hunger emerge to force us to look at our organizational design. The question "What are we trying to do?" is replaced by

"Who are we?" This "identity question" helps name the current reality in The United Methodist Church.

Compare the two lists below:

MEANS OF GRACE	CHURCH COMMITTEES
Prayer	Spiritual Life
Study of Scripture	Christian Education
Lord's Supper	Worship
Acts of Mercy	Missions
Fasting/Abstinence	Stewardship
Christian Conference	Evangelism
	Church and Society

Listed on the left are some of the means of grace around which John Wesley designed the early Methodist movement. Listed on the right are the names of various committees in today's church. These committees were created to ensure the practice of the means of grace.

In every generation, the church re-creates the organizational structure so that the work of the church might occur. Leaders make a fundamental commitment to providing a sound structure that will enable a community to practice the means of grace and grow as Christian disciples. Unfortunately, in every generation a subtle, but substantial, shift occurs where the focus turns from the practice of spiritual disciplines to the maintenance of the institutional structure. More time is given to meetings than to accomplishing the tasks the meetings are called to perform. The church is inundated in elections, agendas, minutes, meetings, councils, and votes. Congregations are characterized by talk rather than action; meetings rather than ministry; and planning rather than praying. Worship becomes more like performance art; education is more academic and less experiential; and "missions" is what is *given to* rather than *participated in*. The church compares itself to a business and becomes preoccupied with numbers and statistics. Ultimately, the work of the church becomes institutional maintenance and survival, not the spreading of the gospel.

Many people view this condition as cause for despair, and they lament the situation. Although it is cause for alarm, and it calls us to action; it is not the disaster some claim. The church has been here before; in Methodism at least twice — once just prior to the Civil War and again shortly after the turn of the twentieth century. Currently, the church is revisiting a phase in a cycle. By adopting a systems view of our church's history, we can see better where we are by looking at how we got here.

Chapter Two Questions

1. In what ways does a focus on "institutional structure" displace Christian community? At its best, how might the institutional structure empower and enable Christian community?
2. What practices make Christians (particularly United Methodists) unique and of value in our culture?
3. How widespread are the practices of personal devotion (individual) and the means of grace (corporate) in your church? How might these practices be better supported?
4. How well do the members of your congregation know and understand their Wesleyan heritage and history? How might this knowledge and understanding be improved? What value is there in knowing this history and heritage?

Chapter Three:
To the Present Day

O ne word characterizes the twentieth century better than any other does: change. Scan this partial list of the discoveries, inventions, and changes of the past fifty years.[1]

1950s	
Credit cards	Computer hard disk
Polio vaccine	Integrated circuits
Super Glue	Phone answering machines
Rock and Roll	Dodgers and Giants
DNA	move to west coast
Radial tires	Brown vs. Board of Education
Teflon™	Modem
Oral contraceptives	Ultrasound
TV dinners	Electrocardiograph
Microchip	Pacemakers
Pop-top cans	Power steering
Hula Hoop	Mr. Potato Head
Fiber optics	

1960s	
Artificial heart	Word processor
Audio cassettes	Videodiscs
Lunar landing	Acid rain
Breast implants	Valium

Soft contact lenses
Computer mouse
Ibuprofen
Miniskirts
John Kennedy, Robert Kennedy,
Martin Luther King, Jr. assassinations
The Beatles
Liver, lung, and heart transplants
Touch-tone phones

Instant color film
Astroturf
Aspartame
Coronary bypass
Civil rights
Permanent-Press
Holograms
Virtual reality

1970s

Floppy disks
Test-tube baby
Compact discs
Daisy-wheel, dot matrix,
ink-jet, and laser printers
Ethernet
Neutron bomb
Personal computer
Computer/video games
Kevlar

Watergate and Nixon's resignation
OPEC oil embargo
Disco
Food processors
Space stations
Gene-splicing
Post-It™ notes
Synthetic blood
VHS video

1980s

Cloning of fish
MS-DOS
Cellular phones
Computer viruses
Digital audiotape
CD-ROM
Rubik's Cube
Macintosh computers
Random Access Memory (RAM)
AIDS identified
Berlin Wall falls

Chernobyl
Prozac
Soy milk
Computer animation
Stealth bombers
Doppler radar
Disposable contact lenses
Microsoft Windows
Desktop publishing
Fetal surgery
World Wide Web

1990s	
End of Apartheid	Web TV
Instant language translators	Commercial electric cars
Pentium processors	Java computer language
"Intelligent" metal	HIV protease inhibitor
(hardens under stress)	Break-up of the USSR
The Chunnel	Antimatter created in
Cloning of sheep	controlled setting

These changes are presented in random order intentionally. Change is fast, furious, chaotic, and constant. It is difficult to know what the next change will be and what impact it will have on our lives. Once we adjust to the changes that occur, we rarely wish the changes would go away.

In the 1970s, biologist Gregory Bateson identified two "orders" of change: first- and second-order change.[2] First-order change is reversible change — where something new or different occurs before things return to their original state. Some people find dieting to be first-order change. The dieter changes eating and exercise habits for a time and loses weight; but the dieter returns to old habits and regains the weight. A symbol of first-order change is a pendulum.

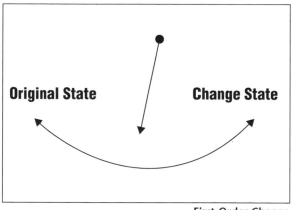

Original State　　**Change State**

First Order Change

Second-order change is irreversible. Once the change occurs, it is impossible to return to the former state. Aging is second-order change. As much as we might like to reverse the effects, it is impossible. A symbol of second-order change is an arrow. (See page 24.)

I would like to propose a third order of change — a synthesis of both first- and second-order change. *Third-order change is returning to where we started — for the very first time.* Although this sounds contradictory, it means that we return to a particular environment (first-order change) that has undergone irreversible transformation (second-order change). I recently visited the farmland that once belonged to my grandparents and found it developed. Shopping centers, fast-food restaurants, a car wash, and a sports

Second-Order Change

complex occupied the land that once yielded crops and livestock. The terrain was familiar, but the changes were startling. During my youth, I walked that land thousands of times, but now it is different. A symbol for third-order change is a spiral (see the illustration below).

The third order of change helps explain the current reality of The United Methodist Church. The challenges that face the church today are similar to conditions it has encountered before. We have returned to issues of membership loss, attendance declines, financial hardships, and ethical debates; but we live in an entirely different cultural paradigm.

It is important to take a "systems approach" to the history of our church. Recent books and articles point to the rapid decline in membership and attendance in Methodist churches over the past forty years. Following almost two hundred years of numerical growth, the Methodist Church experienced a turnaround. These measurements were made in real numbers, and they tell one story. However, when these numbers are converted to percentage of population, they indicate that the decline began in the middle of the nineteenth century, interrupted by infrequent periods of brief growth. In reality, the growth and decline of the Methodist Church has gone through a series of cycles, each only slightly different from the last.

Third-Order Change

Prior to the Civil War, the Methodist Church engaged in social and political debate around the issues of slavery and states' rights. Politics took center stage, and many pulpits became platforms for speech making. The church became polarized over political issues, and spiritual development and outreach receded into the background. Individuals looking for spiritual community who were not interested in the political agendas of the various factions found that there was no place left for them in the church.

Following the Civil War, the country moved toward reconciliation and reconstruction. The Methodist Church joined this movement. Disillusioned with the institutional infighting prior to the war, leaders of the church shifted the focus from structure to rebuilding spiritual community. A renewed commitment to developing strong Christian churches motivated Methodism to begin forming new congregations across the country and to extend mission outreach around the world. This fever to spread scriptural holiness across the land helped to usher in the Third Great Awakening. By the turn of the century, Methodism had recovered much of its pre-Civil War energy. As the church grew stronger in numbers and influence, new organizational structures were designed. As the structures became more complex and as congregations grew larger, more attention was shifted from building community to maintaining the organization. Toward the end of the second decade of the twentieth century, membership reached a plateau and began to decline. Once again, pulpits became centers for political posturing concerning the role of America in the first World War. The church lost its center.

After the war and the onset of the Great Depression, America entered a period of community building based upon shared values of kindness, mercy, hope, and justice. The Methodist Church stepped forward to provide leadership. Completely redesigning existing structures, the church renewed its commitment to taking the good news of Jesus Christ into the world. New churches were created in the forty eight states, and world mission giving reached an all-time high. Membership (in real numbers) picked up, and attendance was consistently strong.

With strength came the need for new structures. Our present-day committee structures were developed throughout this period. During the 1950s and '60s, the focus shifted from the formation of faith communities to the development of organizational structures. Growth peaked, then reversed. By the end of the 1960s, the church involved itself in the politics of the Vietnam War. Polarization inevitably followed, exacerbating the acceleration of decline. With the merger of The Methodist Church and the Evangelical United Brethren in 1968, more focus was turned to structure, organization, and polity, leaving even less attention to faith formation and spiritual development.

Today, we are awakening to the need to return to our spiritual center. The structures created following World War II are no longer appropriate. In fact, they may actually prevent us from attending to the real work of the church. Spiritual hunger and a seeking after truth characterize our culture, yet many people feel that the church is ill equipped to respond. One assessment is that the Christian church is out of synch with people's needs.

A cycle theory helps explain how the church moved out of touch with people. Both churches and individuals are located along two continua: (1) doing and

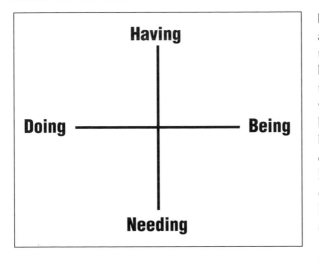

being, and (2) having and needing. In the continuum of doing and being, doing relates to the activities in which we engage; whereas, being relates to the beliefs, values, and principles by which we live. Each person and each organization finds health where being and doing are balanced.

In the second continuum, having and needing, having reflects more than just possessing material things. It involves a sense of security, control, well being, and affluence. Needing reflects feelings of anxiety, uncertainty, deprivation, and limitation.

Placing the two continua together as horizontal and vertical axes creates four quadrants that define separate states: *having-doing*, *needing-doing*, *needing-being*, and *having-being*.

People and organizations in the *having-doing* state define reality by engaging in activities and channeling resources to accomplish tasks. Beyond achieving physical wealth, people in this state have a sense of possibility and promise. People gain a sense of well being from being actively involved in work that is meaningful. People and organizations who operate from a *having-doing* perspective are happiest when they are busy and productive.

People operating out of the *needing-doing* state define their reality by engaging in activities determined and limited by the management of available resources. People and organizations turn their attention from what they have to what they lack. Their time and effort are geared toward raising funds and juggling demands. They lower expectations to match finite supplies, and they define success by doing as much as possible with as little as possible. People and organizations in the state of *needing-doing* find satisfaction in accomplishing what they can to the best of their abilities.

People and organizations in the *needing-being* state define reality as a focus on improvement, growth, values clarification, and visioning in a time of uncertainty and limited available resources. People and organizations struggle with identity issues as they redefine their purpose. Their activities are limited by a lack of resources and an absence of vision. Their focus turns inward. They find it difficult to achieve satisfaction because their search for identity is hampered by their sense of need.

People and organizations in the *having-being* state define reality as balance: individuals and organizations feel that they have the resources needed to thrive and the time and space necessary to focus on identity issues, learning, and improvement. With this attainment of balance comes a desire to put beliefs, knowledge, and principles into action. People and organizations in the having-being state achieve satisfaction by moving toward doing.

Every person and every organization experiences all four states at one time or another. When individuals and organizations experience the same state at the same time, the connection provides mutual strength. In the 1950s, both people and the church experienced the state of *having-doing*. The postwar society was full of new opportunities. People felt a sense of affluence as they purchased homes and cars, appliances, televisions, stereos, and generally experienced a standard of living previously unknown. People prized leisure time; and they engaged in hobbies, activities, and vacations with energy. They were busy and enjoyed a high level of contentment. Even in the shadow of Cold War anxiety, people felt hopeful and happy.

During this same period, the Methodist Church — and the Evangelical United Brethren Church with which it would merge in 1968 — was characterized by a high level of activity. Sunday schools were bursting, worship attendance was high, fellowship activities were plentiful, and mission involvement was at an all-time peak. To keep pace with the boom in activity, churches created elaborate organizational structures to support the work. Giving of money and time was plentiful, and the greatest worry was how to use everything. New buildings were built, old buildings were renovated, and the future looked bright.

The downside to growth was a shift toward a maintenance mentality that still prevails in the church. More money and resources were needed to support the burgeoning structures of the Methodist Church. Demands for staff, facilities, and connectional and pastoral support increased, forcing cuts in available funds for program and missions. Institutional costs escalated each year, while mission and program monies diminished.

During the 1950's, people were attracted by churches involved in activities that helped them live out of their sense of personal mission and values. Growing disciples looked to the church to give them opportunities to serve, learn, and give. As mission and program opportunities receded in the 1960s and '70s, so did the interest of many people. Both the church and the people turned their attention inward, but in significantly different ways.

The people felt a void. The church no longer provided nurture and support for their personal growth. Culturally, times were growing less certain and more threatening. Economic crises and growing disillusionment with institutions and government were pervasive. By the late 1970s and early 1980s, people started seeking meaning in new places and exploring new avenues of spiritual growth. The influence of the church decreased. People shifted from the *having-doing* state into the *needing-doing* state during the 1970s and '80s, before settling into the *needing-being* state in the 1990s.

Concurrently, the church found itself supporting a complex hierarchical structure with diminishing human and material resources. Doing *with* less meant doing less. The identity of the church was threatened, and leaders turned their attention to patching and reupholstering its damaged credibility. Missions and evangelism were hurt most during the late 1970s and early 1980s as outreach ministries seriously diminished — to be picked up by numerous para-church organizations. New church starts were few and far between. New missions were infrequent, and support for long-standing missions disappeared. Theologically, the church was perceived as standing for little and believing anything. Still defining itself by activity and organization, the church shifted from the *having-doing* state to the *needing-doing* state, where it found itself by the mid-1990s.

The relationship between the church — *needing-doing* — and the people — *needing-being* — explains where we are today. The church is realizing that it is not in synch with the people. The people are struggling with the identity issues of "Who are we?" and "What are we doing here?" The church has been struggling with how to do its work without taking time to revisit its own identity issues. Had the church been more attentive to the core values and shared visions of its members, it would have realized long ago why its activities were no longer attractive. A healthy relationship cannot exist between needy organizations and needy individuals. If the church is to have meaning in the lives of men and women, it must offer them a way to address identity issues from a position of strength. In other words, the church needs to shift into a *having-being* state, where its time, energy, and resources are channeled toward spiritual growth, faith formation, and empowering Christian discipleship.

This shift is already occurring. Small groups, renewed interest in spiritual gifts and the practice of the means of grace, seeker-friendly worship, and a growing sense of partnership between laity and clergy are hopeful signs that the church is breaking away from structures that are no longer appropriate. Many congregations are turning their attention from what they don't have and cannot do toward what they do have and can accomplish. A new flexibility is emerging, and the focus is on building community, not on preserving the institution.

The graphic on page 29 helps illustrate where we are by tracing where we have been. It illustrates how we have moved through the historical cycles, and it supports the argument that the time is right to reclaim the Jesus model of the church and to refocus on the means of grace.

We are currently poised to experience a third-order change in The United Methodist Church. Individuals seeking a clear sense of identity and purpose are looking for a church that is focused on building relationships with God and neighbor. Developing this kind of church is a major paradigm shift that returns us to our roots while moving us to a place we have never been. It is not enough

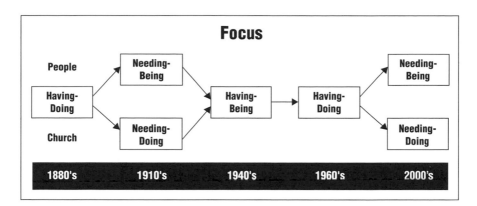

to know where we have come from; it is imperative to see where we stand in relationship to this emerging paradigm. A clear picture of current reality is needed.

Chapter Three Questions

1. Why does an organization's focus tend to shift from mission and purpose to structure and organization?
2. How does it affect your thinking to see this shift as part of a natural and normal cycle instead of a linear negative trend? How can understanding the cyclical nature of organizational life help you plan and prepare for the future?
3. As a culture, where would you place us on the having-needing/doing-being chart? Where would you place your congregation? How do they relate?
4. What are the implications for your congregation to move from where it is now to the having-being state? (If you are already in the having-being state, how have you gotten here? How do you maintain balance?)

Section 2

Where Are We Now?

Chapter Four:
Where We Are in Time

Frame. Focus. Click. You have a snapshot. Taking a picture of our current reality gives us a starting point. However, time keeps rolling on. In no time at all, the picture is out of date. As we examine our snapshot of current reality, we need to keep in mind that we must take new "pictures" all the time. Current reality is a moving target. Current can mean either "right now" or "the direction of the flow." For our purposes, both definitions apply.

Look at the illustration below. It is a way of naming our current reality based on the information from the first three chapters.

A SHIFT OF PARADIGM		
THE ACTIVITY-CENTER PARADIGM		THE FAITH-FORMING COMMUNITY PARADIGM
The Church	FOCUS	Jesus Christ
Initial Assent	DECISION	Journey
Time, Talent, and Treasure	REQUIREMENTS	Practice of Spiritual Disciplines
Individual	ACCOUNTABILITY	Small Group
Professional Staff	MINISTERS	The People
Within a Building	LOCATION	In the World

The paradigm shift noted above is not a statement of what ought to be; it simply names what is. Whether it is good or bad, right or wrong, is not the point. The activity-center paradigm characterized The United Methodist Church and its antecedents for the better part of the last fifty years. In its time, it served the church well. In today's world, it is no longer appropriate.

In the membership boom following World War II, the church took center stage as the focus of organized religion. Joining the church meant making a one-time commitment to "uphold the church by prayer, presence, gifts, and service." Once these promises were made, the individual decided to what extent he or she would keep them. For the most part, church members learned to put their money in the collection plate and let the "hired professionals" perform the ministries of the church. The ministries of the church were referred to as its "programs," and they were planned and performed by various committees. The church, as defined in popular usage, was the *place* you went. For a great number of Americans, this description of the church fits their current perception perfectly.

However, a shift is occurring. People are not as insistent that their churches be activity centers. "Belonging" no longer means inclusion in a club or organization, but connection in community. As one woman remarked, "There is a big difference between being a part in a machine and being an organ in the human body. For years, I felt like I was part of a machine; now I'm looking for something more warm and alive." This is the distinction between the old and the new paradigm: the move from a mechanistic model to an organic model — from institution to community. Rather than developing a relationship to the church, people are seeking relationships with Jesus Christ and with others. No longer is "becoming a member" of the church a one-time event; instead, participation in the community of faith requires a commitment to take a journey. The journey upholds the institution as a means to an end, instead of as an end in itself. We no longer uphold the church by prayers, presence, gifts, and service; but we engage in the spiritual disciplines — including the means of grace — to grow as Christian disciples and to strengthen and nurture the Christian community. With the focus on community building comes a deeper sense of accountability to the group. Small groups are attractive to people as a way to make the journey and to practice the spiritual disciplines. Together, all people find their gifts and calling and enter into the ministry of the church. The church is no longer where we go, but who we are.

This emerging paradigm confirms the trends named earlier. Today's faith communities are combining the Jesus and Pauline models of the church. Centering on the means of grace and the practice of the classic spiritual disciplines moves us away from corporate organizational structures toward new models of ministry that celebrate our Wesleyan roots. The evolution of activity-center churches into faith-forming communities moves us from the *needing-doing* state into the *having-being* state. It readies us to meet people who are on a spiritual quest, but who are disillusioned with a church that has long been inwardly focused. All these factors are converging to create a new possibility for the church. We have an opportunity to be a new kind of church.

Naming the paradigm shift is helpful, but we need to examine the "snap-shot" more closely. As we look more carefully, we notice a lot of blurred edges — things keep moving, and they don't sit still to be photographed. The old paradigm is moving out; the new paradigm is moving in. Our current reality is an in-between time. We live in a reality where the old and new paradigms both exist — often in conflict.

Many people defend the old paradigm by saying that it contains the new paradigm. They say that the new paradigm isn't really new at all and that there is no reason to change anything. Comments such as, "Our church has had small groups for years" or, "I have always viewed my spirituality as a journey" or, "We print in our bulletin each week that the ministers of the church are its members" dismiss the paradigm shift and defend the way things are. This is a subtle, but potentially dangerous, form of resistance.

There are four questions to consider as "reality checks" that help to clarify the difference between what is emerging and what we are already experiencing.

1.   Do we primarily invite people to support the institutional church, or do we invite them into relationship with Jesus Christ?

2.   Do we primarily define the church by the programs it offers, or do we define the church by its fundamental beliefs?

3.   Do we provide opportunities for faith formation and spiritual development to the individual, or do we design these opportunities to be corporate experiences as well?

4.   Do we primarily view the church as a place that serves the people who come, or do we see the church as people who gather together to be sent forth to serve others?

The church exists to fulfill its primary task: to reach out and receive people in the name of Jesus Christ, relate people to God, nurture and strengthen people in their faith and life, and send them into the world to lead transformed and transforming lives. Maturing Christian disciples will engage in many forms of service; however, assigning someone to a committee or to a position of leadership is no guarantee that he or she will progress on the journey of faith. Everyone needs opportunities to put faith into action, but the church's focus must be on the whole of the primary task. The church is the place where people develop and strengthen their relationship with Jesus Christ. Church programs and practices that involve people in work that does not add to their growth as disciples are inappropriate and misdirected. People are not intended to serve the institution of the church. The institution is intended to provide people with everything they need to be the church.

The church is always more than the programs it provides. What a church does is determined by its identity, not the other way around. When I moved to Nashville, Tennessee, I went to a number of churches as I sought a spiritual community. Many pastors and lay members of various local congregations visited my home to encourage me to return to their churches. When I asked the question "Why should I become a member of your faith community?" the answers I received mainly had to do with programs offered. The majority of people responded by telling me what their church does, not by helping me understand who they are as a congregation. When I pushed the visitors to tell me why their churches offered the programs they do, most were unable to elaborate. One young woman, though, described her church as a gathering of people journeying together to discover the most appropriate ways to be obedient to God's will. Her perception of the church is that of a discovery center where seekers after God come to know Jesus Christ and one another in deep and meaningful ways. In a full hour of discussion, this woman only rarely mentioned programs. Her focus was on the relationships that built community in her church.

The programs that a church offers are like the fruit on a healthy tree: the healthier the tree, the more fruit. Focusing on the fruit won't keep the tree healthy. Nurture, pruning, tending, and feeding the tree yields the fruit. Many churches appear healthy because of the amount of "fruit" they bear, while the tree itself is in ill health. Over time, the programs suffer decline, the church dwindles — the fruit disappears — and no one understands why.

The tree image offers another important learning. The tree is a complex system of interdependent parts. Roots sink deep into the soil to receive water and nutrients, sending food through the cells of the trunk into the branches, which yield leaves and fruit. Information courses throughout the system to direct, distribute, and store the necessary components for the different parts of the tree. If any part of the tree becomes separated from it, it ceases to be the tree. A leaf, a fruit, a branch, or a root that is severed is dead. Life depends on connection.

This is also true in the church. One of the most significant dangers facing our church today is that so many people view membership in a community of faith as personal, private, and optional. The individual makes the rules and determines his or her level of involvement. Historically, all instruction given to the church was corporate. The people of God were understood as a single entity. When Jesus taught *"you* are the light of the world," "I will not leave *you* orphaned," the "you" was always plural. The hymnody of the church was predominantly corporate until the nineteenth century, when personal pietism transformed the way people viewed their relationship with God. *A Mighty Fortress is Our God* gave way to *I Walk Through the Garden Alone. Now Thank We All Our God* succumbed to *Blessed Assurance Jesus Is Mine!*

Throughout our Judeo-Christian history, the interconnection of the community has been fundamental. The transgression of one individual was the transgression of all. No "sin" was ever just the problem of the "sinner"; it was a concern of the community in which the sin occurred. The Hebrew people defined themselves by this standard, but this standard was also true for the earliest Christian church, the Roman Catholic Church, the Eastern Orthodox Church, and the early Protestant movement. It is only in recent history that the communal nature of the church has diminished. As we move into the twenty-first century, the communal nature of the church is reemerging. When one part of an organism is affected, the whole organism is affected. Interconnection is at the heart of the church. Christian growth and spiritual formation is a corporate act. When faith development is practiced as an individual act, it loses much of its power. Indeed, the classical spiritual disciplines that John Wesley held forth as means of grace were all corporate. Prayer with and for others; the celebration of the Lord's Supper; making sense of the Scriptures; Christian conversation; the performance of acts of mercy; covenants of abstinence and fasting — all these practices required community. The very nature of the class and band meetings was corporate. John Wesley's teachings make it clear that spiritual people are those who are connected to God and to one another. There is no such thing as a solitary Christian. For these reasons and many others, it is imperative that we adopt a systems-thinking approach to the church.

Furthermore, men and women embark on the journey of Christian discipleship to learn to serve others. The very nature of the church is different from almost every other organization. While most organizations exist to serve their members, the church exists as an organization to serve nonmembers. Evangelism, mission work, healing and compassion, servanthood, and apostleship are just a few of the key characteristics of the church that illustrate this truth. The church is not a service agency where people come to have their needs met. Certainly this happens, but it happens as one phase of a transformation process that takes individuals and knits them together in a faith-forming community. This community, the body of Christ, exists to bring light, love, and healing into the world through the gospel of Jesus Christ. The church focuses inward to be empowered to focus outward. If it settles for mere inward focus, it loses its unique identity.

Church leaders who say that their churches are already living in the faith-forming-community paradigm often see themselves as being effective at one or two aspects of the primary task — usually relating people to God and nurturing and strengthening them in their faith journeys. They say that they have small groups for growth and development or that they have vital worship or education opportunities, and they believe that they are positioned squarely in the newly emerging paradigm. However, in the new paradigm, the primary task of the church is not four separate ministry functions; instead, it is one process with four clearly discernible phases. Just as each year involves four distinct seasons that follow one another in the same pattern, so the primary task involves all four phases. We do not fulfill the primary task unless we attend to the whole process. To focus on one or two aspects of the primary task has as much validity as deciding to allow only spring and summer to define a year. Churches centered squarely in the new paradigm are focused on people in relationship to God, to one another, and to the world. The ministry is an enabling ministry that helps individuals discover their gifts and understand their place in the corporate body of Christ. While meeting the needs of the community as it learns and grows, the ultimate concern in the new paradigm is the transformation of the world.

Awakening to a Brave New World

The world that the church is attempting to transform is a different world from what it was just one generation ago. Although the church travels through cycles, and many of the issues we are dealing with today have been dealt with many times in the past, the tools we have to deal with them today are very different. Naming our current reality requires that we understand the digital age in which we live.

Information, knowledge, and technology — especially computer technology — make today's world very different from anything anyone has experienced. Our ability to process information and communicate it to all corners of the globe is phenomenal. Each day, the limit to what humankind can accomplish diminishes. Our capacity for both good and ill grows geometrically. In many cases, what we can accomplish far outstrips our ability to understand the implications of what we are doing. As our mastery of science, nature, and technology increases, we have even greater need of a sound spiritual center. As the turbulent, white-water-rapids rate of change sweeps us along, the church has a unique role to play in bringing people balance, comfort, vision, and strength. Although science and technology redefine our reality almost by the hour, they are not our ultimate concern. There is something more — something greater — that gives meaning and purpose to human lives. The gospel message and the God who makes all things possible — these are our ultimate concerns, and the church offers us the opportunity to refocus and regain perspective.

Cultural observers have labeled today's world, "postmodern." In popular usage, postmodernism refers to a philosophy that questions everything, believes nothing absolutely, is subjective, deconstructs everything to fundamental parts, distrusts institutions, and relates to people and things based on function instead of values. This cultural milieu is where The United Methodist Church and other religious institutions find themselves today.

Throughout its history, The United Methodist Church (and, indeed, the entire Christian church) has been secure in its position in society. Until the latter half of the twentieth century, the church was looked upon as trustworthy and true, morally and ethically sound, inspired by God, and deserving of devotion and honor. To question the church, at any level, was unacceptable. For centuries, the church had the power and authority to quell any and all challenges to its position within society. However, the church's identity as the keeper of truth and the font of wisdom eroded under the onslaught of thinkers such as Copernicus, Newton, Darwin, Freud, and Einstein. Ironically, Johann

Gutenberg, the inventor of movable type, dealt the church its most devastating blow when he made the Bible available to people beyond the inner academic circles of church leaders. New ideas and incredible challenges to orthodox belief spread quickly, but the church simply held to an "it's-true-because-we-say-so" position. The church damaged its credibility; and as the postmodern spirit prevailed, many people lost faith in the institutional church altogether. Today, there is a great division between those who feel that postmodern thinking is a threat to the survival of the church and those who feel that postmodernism might be the church's salvation.

Postmodernism calls into question the very nature of the institution, asking whether there is even a need for the institutional church. In postmodern thought, wherever like-minded, like-hearted people gather together is where you find church. Postmoderns challenge a wide variety of sacred assumptions of the institutional church. Many people in this postmodern age are seeking meaning rather than answers. They seek relevancy rather than truth. They want to be involved in ministry instead of working for the church. Moreover, they will listen to any voice that moves them in these directions. Unless The United Methodist Church sees the postmodern age as our current reality instead of as a problem to be solved, it very well may lose what credibility it retains.

Being a church in the postmodern era means being a new kind of church. As leaders, we need great courage to allow people to question basic tenets and beliefs; but if we honestly believe what we say we do, then there is no threat. Current controversies about polity and doctrine, the integrity of Scripture, the acceptability of certain types of people for ordination, the church's relationship to people with alternative sexual preferences, among others, indicate that our view of God is too small and that our reverence for the institutional church is too great. Any challenge to the "truth" is a threat only to the extent that God isn't big enough to handle it.

MODERNISM FOCUSES ON:	POSTMODERNISM FOCUSES ON:
Answers	Questions
Truth	Relevancy
Personal relationships	Functional relationships
Trust	Skepticism
Success	Wholeness
Family (biological)	Family (functional)

Postmodern thinkers are calling for the institutional church to refocus on what is most important. They want to know who Jesus Christ is, what relevancy a relationship with Jesus can have in their lives, what it means to journey and learn together, and what it means to discover their full potential. Postmodern thinkers have often been labeled a people without values. This is a false label. The postmodern age has values, but they are different from the values of past generations.

These two lists illustrate just a few differences between modernism and postmodernism, and they reveal that our current United Methodist Church is designed to meet the needs and support the values of the modern era. The good news is that the church is responding to the paradigm shift to postmodernism as relevancy, wholeness, and small-group connection are becoming more important. The postmodern era is having an influence on The United Methodist Church, but more by default than by design. The time has come — indeed it is already past — for the church to stop resisting the paradigm shift and to begin strategizing the best way to minister within it effectively.

Another benefit of postmodern thinking is the realization that many of our cultural constructs are false. To postmodern thinkers, there is no first world and third world, no gay and straight, no upper- and lower-class. There is one world, one humanity, one quality of person. We are a global community, and the barriers and distinctions that separate us are wrong, harmful, and fundamentally evil. Postmodernism calls us to examine carefully where we are in the world.

Chapter Four Questions

1. Thinking of the majority of members in your church (not just the key leaders or most active participants), what percentage "live" in the Faith Community Paradigm? What percentage are in the Activity Center paradigm? How are needs met for both segments of the congregation?

2. Which of the two paradigms exerts the most influence over the other? How is this a healthy tension? Where does it pose problems?

3.Take time in a group to answer and explore the four questions on page 37.

Chapter Five:
Where We Are in the World

The world — and our place in it — is constantly changing in fundamental ways. In 1991, the war in the Persian Gulf came into our living rooms in real-time. We watched the war as it happened. Within days, Americans learned more about the Middle East than most had ever known. Sound bites, images, opinions, and analysis shaped whole new ways of thinking and seeing. A decade later, the terrorist attacks on September 11 once more altered millions of people's perceptions about the world. Complacency gave way to anxiety, faith was tested by fear, and for many people the world became a very different place. Global communications, the Internet, and travel continue to shrink our world. It grows ever more difficult to stay ignorant of other peoples and places. Daily we are confronted and challenged by other cultures, other religions, and other worldviews. Some find this threatening, but for the people of God, this provides a rich and exciting opportunity to learn, grow, and serve. The lines between "us" and "them" are blurring. By God's grace and guidance, perhaps we might learn to see beyond our differences to extend the hand of Christ in fellowship to all people and find better ways to relate than destructive violence. The church has a potentially significant role to play in such a shift.

How does this current reality affect The United Methodist Church? One representative from the United Methodist General Board of Global Ministries reports that we are living in a paradox: total dollar giving to foreign missions is growing, although the percentage of money we are giving to foreign missions is declining; and fewer people know where the money goes. A fairly large United Methodist Church in Florida supports two missionaries to Kisangani, Africa. Although the church has been supporting the couple for more than ten years, only two out of the more than one hundred people present at a recent dinner could point out Kisangani on a map. For the most part, our sense of connection to the world is tenuous at best, and our involvement consists of making contributions to the church and other agencies that do work in other parts of the world. In The United Methodist Church, there is only a small segment of people who understand that we are part of a global community and a universal church. What happens to other people in other lands is not a primary focus in most of our churches today.

This is not to say that Methodism is not alive and well in the world. The Methodist church is booming around the globe, even as it declines in North America. Sadly, this is news to most United Methodists. The fact that the majority of the members of our denomination have no idea what is happening in the church around the world indicates just how far out of step we are with the current paradigm. There is no "over there," but the church has yet to catch on.

The lack of awareness of the world church, of which we are a part, opens the door to a kind of imperialism. The way church is experienced in North America has become "normal," what people think church ought to be. Resources (such as this one) are written from a white-Anglo, North American perspective for a predominantly white-Anglo, middle-class audience. Although it is vitally important to produce these resources, it is important to keep in mind that we are speaking to only one segment of the church, and today *the white-Anglo segment is the minority segment.* The cultural and church paradigm shifts discussed in this book are important across racial, ethnic, and geographic lines; but the meaning of, and response to, these shifts will be very different.

Not only is it important that we begin developing resources for the entire global church, but — even more important — we must open ourselves to the many ways that the global church can resource and teach us. The North American white, middle-class way is not the only way. Other practices, rituals, ways of relating to God and community, praying, and praising are valid; and they can help us grow in our own relationship with God. The Methodist Church of the modern era had a lot to *teach.* In the postmodern era, we have a lot to *learn.*

That there is ignorance about our current global reality should not surprise us when we consider that many of us are not even aware of the things happening in our own communities.

Due to construction on a major highway, I detoured through a suburb of Philadelphia. Lost and confused, I found myself in a neighborhood that looked like a war zone. Buildings were crumbling, all the windows were boarded up or covered with sheets, broken glass and garbage littered sidewalks, and the streets were clogged with filth. Burned out husks of cars lined the curbs. Street signs were torn down, graffiti covered every wall and vehicle, and bars covered every doorway. People inhabited these dwellings. The assault on my suburban sensibilities was immense. I pride myself about being generous to ministries for the homeless, the hungry, and the hurt. I make certain that I set aside money to support this important work, but I do it from the safety of my apartment; and I contribute money through the collection at my local church. Until I "got lost," I didn't have to confront the reality of the situation.

The church exists in a broken world. The United States of America still ranks as one of the most affluent nations on earth, but it is also the home of abject poverty, incredible violence, and enormous injustice and inequality. Within easy reach of every United Methodist congregation are literally thousands of people in need of love, caring, and good news, not to mention food, shelter, and clothing. A serious question for each congregation to ask on a regular basis is, "On Sunday morning, would we most likely find Jesus in the pew or on the street?" As the paradigm shifts, the message is clear: people don't need to be "in church"; the church needs to be "in the world."

The personal pietism movement of the nineteenth and early twentieth centuries created a serious dilemma for us. Pietism rightly teaches the importance of prayer, study, fasting, worshiping, giving, and self-control; but pietism is centered in the individual and her or his relationship to God. Piety is an end in itself, and there is no motivation to move beyond a private faith. The popular injunctions of the seventies and eighties to "get right with God" and to know Jesus "as your personal Lord and Savior" reinforced the idea that Christian discipleship was solely between the believer and God. The church became a kind of "filling station," where people went once a week to get replenished for the week to come. A larger vision of a servant community was displaced by the smaller, more provincial vision of having one's own needs met. As one woman very plainly put it, "I'm a nurse. I do for others every day of the week. Sunday is my turn. I go to church for me."

There is nothing wrong with seeking comfort, strength, and spiritual renewal by attending church, but it draws an untenable contrast — either we are in the world or we are in church. Church is seen as a place apart, a port in the storm of the "real world." This sense of retreating from the world to the church is one of the great challenges facing us today. Our primary task clearly defines our faith journey as a continuous cycle of coming to receive so that we go forth to share and serve. True piety prepares us to move beyond ourselves to others in need.

John Wesley was criticized for his focus on the means of grace. Many people perceived them as a way of withdrawing from the world. Prayer, study of Scripture, celebration of the Lord's Supper, Christian conference, and fasting could all take place within the closed community. In answer to these criticisms, Wesley amended his list of the means of grace to include "acts of mercy." Personal piety that fails to move us into service to others was unconscionable to Wesley. "Doing good," "doing no harm," and "attending to all the ordinances of God" were essential provisions of Wesley's general rules of Christian conduct. In Wesley's theology, Christian community formed to spread scriptural holiness across the land. As we share the good news, we begin to experience the kingdom of God. The dynamic relationship of serving and being served was central to Wesley's vision for the church.

There is a great desire in the human heart to be part of something much larger than the self. Even the most needy and broken among us want to serve a greater purpose; we want our lives to have meaning. Daily, people shake their heads and ask, "Is this all there is?" Television, newspapers, radio, and the Internet overwhelm us with images of the way society is breaking down. We are inundated with images of the lowest common denominators of human nature. Crime, violence, disaster, and forecasts of doom pummel us. We need to hear a different kind of message. We need to be part of something that gives us hope, encouragement, and energy. We need to find a place where life feels manageable and where what we say and do matters. Why shouldn't the church be the place where people can hear the message, find the hope, and connect in a meaningful way?

The church is not separate from the rest of the world. Unless we exist as faith-forming communities rooted in and reaching into the world, transformation cannot occur. Our scope, our vision for the church is expanding to global proportions. Stained glass blocks our seeing the world in which we live. Institutional maintenance often gets in the way of ministry. The time has come for leaders at all levels of The United Methodist Church to reevaluate our relationship to our communities, our country, and our world. The world needs healing. The world needs hope. The world needs comfort. The world needs transformation. Isn't it fortunate that the church is exactly what the world needs?

The words of Fred Pratt Green help us to reflect on our need to be connected to the world. Reflect on these lines from the hymn, "When the Church of Jesus."[3]

> When the church of Jesus shuts its outer door,
> lest the roar of traffic drown the voice of prayer,
> may our prayers make us ten times more aware
> that the world we banish is our Christian care.
> If our hearts are lifted where devotion soars
> high above this hungry, suffering world of ours,
> lest our hymns should drug us to forget its needs,
> forge our Christian worship into Christian deeds.
> Lest the gifts we offer, money, talents, time,
> serve to salve our conscience, to our secret shame,
> Lord, reprove, inspire us by the way you give;
> teach us, dying Savior, how true Christians live.*

Chapter Five Questions

1. What are the implications for the Christian faith when the church becomes a "place" people escape to, instead of an "identity" that defines the way they relate to the world?

2. What are some of the ways your congregation helps people understand themselves as the church rather than people who are served by the church?

3. What are some of the ways you equip people to serve others as the body of Christ as they move through their daily lives? How do you evaluate how effectively you do this?

4. What are the concrete and measurable ways that God is using your congregation to transform the world?

Chapter Six:
Where We Are as a Society

Are we more civilized today than we were a generation ago? Do we regard family and community in the same way our parents did? Are the values of today's graduating college seniors similar to the values of the graduates of the 1960s? Are we more materialistic now than we were in the 1950s? Are we more selfish? more giving? healthier? happier? more spiritual?

Everyone has opinions about these questions, but how can we really know? Every day, a newspaper, magazine, or television show presents the latest findings to "prove" that we are taller, shorter, smarter, dumber, prettier, uglier, healthier, sicker (and more gullible) than ever before. We fill our lives with information and ideas; yet the more we hear, the less we know. Politicians, media consultants, newscasters, and even clergy tell us who we are, what to believe, what we need, and how to feel better. Whom do we trust? Ours is a society "tossed to and fro and blown about by every wind of doctrine." (Eph. 4:14, NRSV)

Webster's Dictionary[4] defines "society" as "the totality of social relationships among human beings. A group of human beings bound together by shared institutions and culture." It is mind-boggling to reflect on the implications of such a definition. Think of the number of social relationships in which you engage. Television, computers, air travel, and telecommunications have redefined society within the last generation. The sheer quantity of information that we receive means that we have less time to comprehend and process it. Our beliefs, thinking, and attitudes are influenced by more "social relationships" than ever before. How do we know what we know? In a society that presents so many different perspectives and that changes so constantly, where do we find our center?

The illustrations on page 48 present a simple, but powerful lesson. In an individualistic society such as ours, one person, standing alone, is assaulted by more ideas, influences, and forces than she or he can process. However, in com-

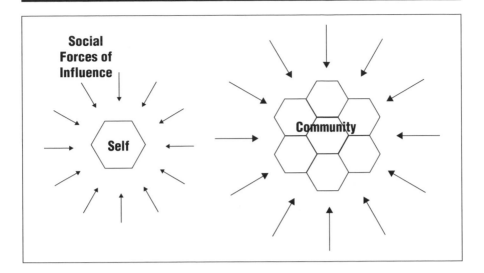

munity we share the burden. No one person is bombarded by all the social messages and forces. In community, we can discuss, disseminate, and even dismiss the information that overwhelms us individually. We are rediscovering the wisdom of "united we stand, divided we fall."

It used to be that our social institutions helped guide us, gave us a sense of place and purpose, and defined for us a mission and an identity. But many people feel that society is breaking down. It may well be that society is merely redefining itself. Regardless of what is happening to our society at large, one person is helpless to deal with all the forces and influences of our social milieu. Alone, we will not survive.

The parallel with the society of Jesus' day is remarkable. The formation of Christian community guaranteed support and encouragement in the face of increasing hostility and violence. The church of Jesus Christ could not have survived without the formation of small communities that prayed, studied, served, and worked together. In fact, these communities were the early church. This church offered a countercultural alternative that called for a new social order.

Where we as the church stand in relationship to our society is ambiguous. The institutional church is revered and derided, respected and held suspect, valued and dismissed by different sectors of our society. People inside the church feel that the church is different from other societal institutions, while outsiders see the church as one institution among many to distrust and avoid. Throughout the history of Christianity, the institutional church has played a prominent role in defining and shaping the moral character of the society. Today, the church no longer fulfills this role.

This is not to say that the church couldn't or shouldn't help to shape societal thinking and values. Before it can happen, however, the church must prove to the world that it has credibility and that it is worthy of being heard. Churches that hold fast to the attitudes and practices of the former paradigm afford themselves little chance to have an impact on society. In our postmodern social climate, credibility is closely linked with relevancy. People need to know what difference it makes to be a disciple of Jesus Christ. Until we communicate in clear, concise, concrete terms how the church makes the world a better place to live, our ability to compete with other social institutions is limited.

There are politicians who tell us that caring for the poor and marginalized is self-defeating and that it perpetuates the problem. Television tells us that we must aspire to a better life, characterized by cars, beer, perfume, the right clothes, the right phone company, and the best toothpaste. Many newscasters describe our society as violent, frightening, dangerous, and corrupt. Various scientists tell us that there is nothing humankind cannot achieve and that science and technology are the keys to solving all our problems. What messages does the church offer in response to these claims? What good are our responses if all we do is talk to ourselves? The mission of our church is no less than the radical transformation of the world. Jesus had every expectation that the church would always offer an alternative message — the good news — to the prevailing "truths" of our world. When we allow society to define the way we live as the church, we lose the power to model a better way.

The organizational structures of most United Methodist congregations are borrowed from the secular world. Committee structures, financial procedures, the recording of minutes, the creation of agendas, the adherence to *Robert's Rules of Order* — all these practices and many others — indicate that society redefines us every bit as much as we redefine it. Dependence on these kinds of practices turns us from our central focus, and it causes us to lose sight of what makes us unique. Ministry is replaced by administration.

This does not mean that we cannot learn important lessons from our culture. In fact, the opposite is true if we hope to make the church an inviting place to those outside our communities of faith. However, the core, the spiritual center, of the church must be firmly in place before we begin borrowing from the secular culture. Then, what we draw into our sphere of reference is shaped by our faith. The shift from an activity-center paradigm to a faith-forming-community paradigm is critical if we are to rediscover our center and create an environment that is fundamentally different from anything else our society has to offer. When the leaders of the institutional church are able to provide something special and unique, we will once again positively affect society and engage in the revolutionary work of Kingdom building.

Defining Our Own Rules

No matter what we do, the relationship of the church to society will change radically in the next few decades. Secular culture will judge us by a simple standard of stewardship: how well we manage our organization. People in the post-modern era tend to be suspicious of success as an indicator of integrity. Much more important is the ability of leaders to keep an institution fresh, innovative, and relevant. The size of a group is less important than how well the leadership can empower the group to engage in meaningful pursuits. Churches that embrace the new paradigm will score high by postmodern standards. Individuals will be encouraged to learn and develop to their fullest potential, while finding opportunities for meaningful service within and beyond a spiritually centered community. Because everyone will be engaged in visioning and planning, participants in the new kind of church will constantly reinvent and redesign it. The focus on Christ, the practice of the means of grace, and the commitment to reach out into the world will confirm the mission of the church, while "new rules" will be developed to enable the community of faith to remain relevant to an ever-changing world.

The leaders of The United Methodist Church stand at an important cross-road. The "game" that we have known and played for years has changed. To play, we need new rules. Either we determine what the rules are, or they will be decided for us. Increasingly, voices from secular society are recommending what the church should do and be. We are being taught religion by Hollywood movie makers and Madison Avenue advertisers. Angels are on TV each week. A recent *New York Times* bestseller described heaven as a computerized, multigalactic corporation. Movies about faith emphasize the supernatural and obscure. This is not a new phenomenon — many people cannot hear a story about Moses without thinking "Charlton Heston." Popular culture has always challenged the church to a certain degree regarding "religious education." Still, in response to articles in *Time* and *Newsweek* about God, angels, and heaven, clergy and lay leaders alike could not discern when the information aligned with the beliefs of their denomination. A promotional brochure for a spirituality retreat crossed my desk that claimed the ordained Methodist retreat leader was a "certified expert in angelology."

Defining the rules that we will live by is not a matter of deciding right and wrong. As a denomination, it is imperative that we share a common understanding of our mission, that we are first and foremost Christian, and that we talk openly and honestly about what we believe and why. A return to our scriptural and theological roots is a first step. It will take courage to confront Scripture with integrity. Many of our dearest and deepest beliefs have nothing at all to do with the Bible. They come to us from carols (i.e., *We Three Kings*. The Gospel of Matthew is the only source for this story, and it does not say anything about kings, the number of travelers, or the orient), legend (there is no direct evidence that Mary Magdalene was a prostitute), film (every popular film about the last hours of Jesus' life depicts Judas going off to hang himself, while the Scriptures give us an option — Matthew, hanging; Acts, falling headlong so that

Judas split open and his insides poured out), and conflation — creating a single story from the four narrative gospels (Jesus is baptized by John in the gospels of Matthew and Mark, but not in the gospels of Luke and John). To read the Bible with integrity, to find out what it really says and means, will take commitment, dedication, and an openness of mind not generally associated with organized religion.

Rediscovering the thought and theology of John Wesley, George Whitfield, Charles Wesley, and others helps clarify our identity. Understanding who we are involves an examination of who we have been in the past. Determining where we want to go in the future requires that we remember our past. Our society cannot provide us this information. We will need to search within our own tradition to find the definition of what it really means to be the church.

Every time a relationship is established, there is a process of mutual discovery. I find out about you, while you find out about me. I disclose information about what I think, feel, believe, and hold sacred. You do the same. As we find common ground — places where we share similar beliefs and values — we develop a bond. Our ability to make disciples of Jesus Christ depends on our ability to form relationships. As members of faith-forming communities, we should be able to communicate clearly what we think, feel, believe, and hold sacred. We should also be listening carefully to the members of our society who are products of the prevailing culture to understand better what they think, feel, believe, and hold sacred. In this way, relationships are formed that can change lives. Once the bonds are forged that create community, the stage is set for spiritual transformation.

Chapter Six Questions

1. What are the challenges you face in helping people put the needs and interests of the community of faith before their own?
2. What are some of the prevailing cultural messages that challenge and contradict some of the central tenets of the Christian faith?
3. What are some of the disadvantages in having the Christian faith defined for us in movies, on television, and in best-selling books? What are some of the benefits?
4. How well are we able to tell our own story? How well do participants in your congregation understand the Bible, the history and tradition of The United Methodist Church, the theology of the church, and the meaning of our symbols and rituals? How might we improve the knowledge of and ability to share our story?

Chapter Seven:
Where We Are as Spiritual Seekers

We tend to think that the church has a monopoly on spirituality. We are wrong. All people are spiritual creatures, whether they are aware of it or not. All people are seeking some source of spiritual fulfillment. Historically, organized religious institutions in Western culture cornered the market on the divine. Options were limited, and variation was slight. The Christian church became a "take-it-or-leave-it" institution. For the most part, people "took it." Over the past thirty years, this paradigm has shifted. An influx of Eastern religious practices, New Age spirituality, fascination with the occult, and a concurrent dissatisfaction with mainline Christianity has broken the field wide open. The Christian church exists in a "buyer's market," where the competition is enormous, expert, and vicious. Mainline Christianity is one selection in a cafeteria of religious choices.

The fundamental question is, "Is the current reality of religious pluralism and 'designer spirituality' a good thing or a bad thing?" If we perceive this current reality as a threat, then we will respond to it in a radically different way than if we perceive it as a positive actuality that is ripe with possibility. It would be simple to point out all the dangers and difficulties of navigating the waters of religious pluralism; mainline religion has taken this approach from time immemorial. Instead, it is helpful to understand where we are, why we are here, and what it may mean for us in the future.

The *New York Times Book Review* best-seller lists in the late 1990s included such titles as *The Celestine Prophecy, Embraced By the Light, Chicken Soup for the Soul, Surfing the Himalayas, Care of the Soul, Conversations with God,* and *The Bible Code.* More recently, *The Prayer of Jabez, The Purpose Driven Life, Your Best Life Now,* and *The Da Vinci Code* have set sales records. Sales of these books suggest a great hunger for things spiritual in our culture. What they have in common is what has become known as "pastiche spirituality," a syncretism of various beliefs and practices from a variety of religious backgrounds and the dominant culture. There is a little of this, a little of that, some traditional orthodoxy sprinkled with some New Age, a dash of Buddhism, some Westernized Sufism, a garnish of science and technology — in short, religion *du jour*. This brand of spirituality is highly subjective, deeply heartfelt, and obviously appealing. Millions of books offering alternative spiritualities are sold each week.

The ease of global communications, the impact of television, the rise of feminist consciousness, the influx of Eastern religions, and the burgeoning explosion of scientific discovery have all contributed to the current reality of religious pluralism. These powerful cultural forces have expedited the paradigm shift, and the mainline Christian churches are only now beginning to understand their impact. The diversity of the people who enter our church doors has never been greater, and their questions of faith have never been more eclectic. The church in the modern world took a defensive posture, making it clear that alternative ways of relating to God were wrong and misguided. Asking questions reflected a lack of faith, and looking into other belief systems was considered a waste of time (and potentially dangerous).

In the postmodern era, where everything is questioned, the church no longer has the luxury of hiding behind its own certitude. The wisdom and integrity of other belief systems; the challenges to patristic, exclusionary structures by women; and the mind-expanding revelations of physics, chemistry, and other sciences all require a different kind of response from the church. In times past, faith without reason condemned the ignorance of the world. The world responded by enlightening itself and exposing faith without reason to be the true ignorance. God is not honored when the church refuses to learn.

The implications for the future are clear. No longer may we rest secure in the understanding of the church as the dispenser of truth. Instead, the church has the potential to be a forum for exploration and discovery — a place where hungry, seeking men and women might journey together on their paths to meaning and relevancy. When the journey is taken with integrity, each person can come to encounter truth in his or her own way, in his or her own time.

The time is ripe for the church to define itself clearly as a place where people can encounter open, honest engagement with issues of faith. Clergy and laity leaders, now more than ever, need knowledge of the Old and New Testaments; the great writings of the mystics, theologians, and reformers of our faith; and the doctrine and polity of the denomination; as well as knowledge about other religions, popular cultural spiritualities, and alternative philosophies. Fewer people will come to the church seeking specific answers to life issues, while more will enter with the hope that the church might offer clarity and focus. The only way the church can do this is for the leaders to be able to engage in thoughtful, informed dialogue with those seeking assistance.

One assumption that can no longer be made in the postmodern era is that people understand Christianity when they come to a Christian church. The

United States has long been considered a "Christian nation," but this is no longer a safe pretext. In the same way that the culture is postmodern, the church culture is post-Christian.

In my last church, a young woman attended services, then remained afterward to talk. She asked me, "Who is Jesus Christ?" I wasn't sure exactly what she was asking, and I even thought she might be joking. It turned out that she had no clue that Jesus Christ was the Son of God, and she didn't know anything about a crucifixion. She was enthralled by the idea of the Bible; and at age 29, she joined the twelve- and thirteen-year-olds in our confirmation class. She grew up in suburban New Jersey, attended public schools, was married with four children, and (in reference to Jesus Christ) claimed that she "had heard the name before"; but her knowledge of Christianity was nonexistent. She claimed that her mother was Catholic and her father was something "that begins with a P." It would be easy to dismiss such stories as anomalies, but more and more people fit into this category. In times past, three categories of belief defined the culture: believers, agnostics (those who aren't sure whether there is a God or not), and atheists (those who are sure that there is no God). A new fourth category is emerging that defines the current reality: ignostics (those who think there must be a "divine something," but who have little or no familiarity with God, Jesus Christ, or the Christian church).

All the searching, seeking, questioning, and doubting are cause for concern in some people's minds. They fear that mainline denominations may not be able to withstand the onslaught of so many challenges. Although the concern is understandable, it is much more likely that the church will benefit and be strengthened by such challenges. This is not the first time that religions have met, clashed, merged, and evolved. What we consider our "Judeo-Christian" heritage contains a synthesis of Egyptian, Hebrew, Babylonian, Greek, Alexandrian, Roman, Byzantine, European, and North American beliefs and practices. What we are experiencing today is just a furthering of the inclusion — bringing Korean, Hispanic, African American, and other influences into the mix. God has been able to withstand such challenges in the past, and it is safe to assume that God will continue to do so in the future.

An often-overlooked benefit of the current passion for the spiritual and the sacred is a recovery of the great writings and teachings of the past. The writings of the church mothers and fathers are being read as never before. The works of such authors as Thomas Moore, while offering superficial presentations of great spiritual thinking, are whetting people's appetites to experience the real thing. "Nonreligious" seekers are more spiritually sophisticated than any other generation, having studied the teachings of a wide variety of classical and contemporary religious writers. The soil is fertile for deep, thorough theological dialogue and reflection, provided the leaders within our churches are up to it.

Cultural indicators point to an amazing opportunity. Ninety-five percent of

Americans in the United States claim to believe in God or a higher power, sixty-two percent of these believe "without a doubt." Seventy-seven percent claim to pray regularly, but only thirty-two percent attend a church weekly.[5] No other institution is more strategically positioned to participate in the faith formation of Americans than the church. Two-thirds of those who are striving to be in relationship with God are inactive or only marginally active with a community of faith. What can we do to reach those who are not currently being served by the church? How can we connect with people as they embark on their journey toward God?

First, the church needs to stop worrying so much about being right. In a relationship, when one person assumes the position of being right, of having all the answers, it puts the other person in the role of being wrong or inferior. The people who are seeking to know God don't need to be corrected. They need to be loved, understood, and cared for. They need to be introduced to the living God, and they need to be offered a vision for their lives that connects them with others in meaningful ways. The rightness of the gospel message and of Christ's church will occur to people as they enter fully into the community of faith. Only when we are unsure of our rightness do we need to keep telling people how right we are.

Second, it is important that we not view different people with different ideas as problems to be solved. Just because a person has different values, beliefs, or lifestyle, doesn't mean that he or she needs to be "fixed." All too often, the church sets a standard for proper Christian conduct that is intended to apply to all people in exactly the same way. Cookie-cutter Christianity denies the complexity of human beings. God made each one of us unique, and God celebrates our diversity. As the people of God, we should enter into this celebration and not seek ways to make everyone think, act, and believe the same. As one young man, when explaining why he left his church, said, "I'm not looking for a place where everyone tells me who I ought to be. I want to find a place where people will help me discover who I really am." Dialogue and intentional listening move us beyond re-creating people in the image we think appropriate to a place of exploration and discovery where we can look to see what God has in mind.

Third, the church makes better use of time and energy focusing on what it does believe rather than on what it doesn't believe. There is only so much time allotted to us on earth; and wasting time in judgment and disapproval prevents us from attending to what is holy, just, and good. If we clarify our mission and focus on our identity as the people of God, we will offer light and hope in the world. Paying attention to what God wants us to do will leave us little time to fuss over what we shouldn't do. Judging the activities of individual members of the community of faith, while interesting and enjoyable for some, does nothing to transform our world into the kingdom of God. When we perpetually lift up the mission of the church, we help people see what they are saved *for*, instead of what they have been saved *from*. Running *toward* a goal is always more compelling than running *from* a punishment.

Finally, the church broadens its appeal as it redefines the primary task in light of the current reality of religious pluralism. Reaching out and receiving people in the name of Christ, relating people to God, nurturing and strengthening people in their faith, and sending them forth to live transformed and transforming lives in the world no longer can be confined to the traditional ways we have engaged in evangelism, worship, education, stewardship, and missions.

Moving beyond traditional definitions is difficult. For many United Methodist congregations, worship is the primary contact point with the community of faith. Evangelism means inviting people to worship; relating them to God, nurturing and strengthening them in the faith, and sending them forth all happens in the context of the sanctuary on Sunday morning. Congregational worship is not what many people are seeking today. Reaching out and receiving are taking on whole new meanings. Some examples of nontraditional ways to reach out and receive are online Internet chat rooms, wine and cheese parties, community clean-up/fix-up parties, interfaith dialogue forums, and Christian dinner theater. Virtually none of these activities occurs within the confines of the church building.

Alternative ways of relating people to God involve the deconstruction of limited images of God. The image of God as Father is powerful and meaningful to many people, but it is not an image that sings in the hearts of everyone. God is much more than any one image that we can devise. Feminist theologians offer us a goddess component long lacking, but greatly needed in our culture. Black theologians challenge our practice of relating people one-on-one with God, rather than in the context of community. Central and South American leaders call us to larger images of God as love and justice. New Age voices point us to God as spirit and energy. Eastern religions remind us that God is in all creation, especially a part of each person we meet. Narrowing the focus to comprehend God is a part of the old paradigm. Expanding our vision is the way of the new paradigm.

Nurturing and strengthening people in their faith requires connection and companionship on the journey. Mentoring, shepherding, small groups, and a rediscovery of the practice of the means of grace all challenge our view of what it means to make Christian disciples. Nurturing and strengthening is not what the church does *for* people, but what it does *with* people. The care and feeding of Christian disciples is a mutual ministry of caring and serving. The community of faith engages in work that benefits the whole, and it leaves no one unattended. Fellowship takes on a whole new meaning.

Sending people into the world is much more than just letting them out the back door, hoping that some part of the Sunday morning message "took hold." People do not leave the church; they are the church. Wherever people move in their daily lives, there the church is represented. Helping people understand the significant role they play in the world is a critical function of the church. This was not a significant function in the modern paradigm. In the postmodern era, however, the church justifies itself only to the extent that it makes a difference. If the church is relevant throughout the week, then it is worth attending so that people might grow, develop, and improve. In the activity-center paradigm, the church was a destination, an end in itself. In the faith-forming-community paradigm, the church is a means to an end, a way of transforming the world.

Our world is alive with spiritual seekers. There is a deep hunger for meaning and connection. Millions of people are on a quest for God. The church is, by its very design, the place where people ought to be able to meet God. We are at a critical juncture in time, part of a global community, in a society filled with both opportunity and peril, where men and women are searching for God. There is no reason why our church buildings shouldn't be hives of incredibly rich activity. The questions that emerge are these: "What do we need to do to become a new kind of church? How can we be faith-forming communities in the new paradigm?"

Currently, most churches are not designed properly to respond to the new paradigm. As the cultural paradigm has shifted, sending everyone back to zero; so too, the church paradigm must shift. Dr. Ezra Earl Jones coined a compelling phrase while he was the General Secretary of the General Board of Discipleship. He says, "The system is designed for the results it is getting," meaning, that what we currently experience — decreasing membership, decreasing attendance, lack of interest, lack of investment of resources — is precisely what we are designed to receive. If we want to get different results, it will require us to create a different system.

Chapter Seven Questions

1. What does it mean to be in ministry "with" people instead of in ministry "to" people or doing ministry "for" people?

2. In what ways do people experience open-mindedness and acceptance when they enter our churches? Where is it absent?

3. Where do people experience inclusion in your church? Exclusion?

4. How can we work to shift our focus from the negative — what we shouldn't do, shouldn't believe, shouldn't allow — to the positive — how to love, serve, accept, and forgive? Why do so many seekers visiting our churches experience negativity?

Section 3

Where Are We Heading?

Chapter Eight:
Systems and Process Thinking

The Apostle Paul presents a compelling metaphor for the church: the Body of Christ. Body imagery powerfully symbolizes the organic, systemic, interrelated nature of the church. Recovery of a "systems" view of the church is critically important in the new paradigm.

A system is an interrelated group of processes that connect to accomplish a particular goal or outcome. Components of systems may include people, resources, raw materials, information, tools, gifts, and skills. Each process in a system uses these component parts as inputs to transform them into something new — outputs.

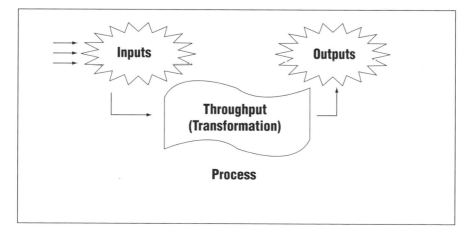

Systems thinking is not difficult, nor is it abstract theory. Life itself is a system, where hundreds of thousands of processes are linked together every day. We have sleeping processes; waking processes; grooming processes; eating, working, playing, and relating processes. We have family systems filled with processes. We have work systems filled with processes. Everything we do is a process that is linked to life systems in some way. Too often, we do not remember that life is a system.

In a system, when one part or process of the system is affected or changed, it affects the entire system. When a person stubs a toe, the entire body reacts to the pain. Systems thinking helps us understand why things happen the way they do, and it makes us more aware of the ways in which our actions affect others.

Jane stops by her secretary's desk on her way to her office. She notices that her secretary, Mark, isn't in yet. Over coffee, Jane remarks to a co-worker, Bob, that Mark is "always late." Bob mentions Jane's remark to his own secretary, Sarah, adding, "he's undependable." Over lunch, Sarah informs Mark that his boss has been spreading the rumor that Mark isn't trustworthy and that he'd better straighten up if he doesn't want to lose his job. When Jane stops by Mark's desk to ask him to take care of some orders, she notices that Mark is very cool and distant toward her. She wanders back into her office, wondering why Mark has such an attitude problem.

What happened? Seeing the entire system, the breakdown in communication is obvious. But each process in the system, taken by itself, yields no clarity about why Mark eventually treats Jane with coldness and distance. How often do we find ourselves in situations where we can only scratch our heads and ponder, "How did this happen?"

This story is an example of a **suboptimized** system. Suboptimization occurs whenever the processes in a system are not aligned toward a common goal. Each process in the saga of Jane and Mark operated independently; and once linked together, they yielded a negative result. Critical information was changed or withheld, communication flowed in a random pattern, and there was no clear purpose to each process.

The goal of every system is **optimization**. Optimization occurs when every process is necessary for reaching the desired goal — there is no extraneous activity or wasted energy. In the case of Jane and Mark, direct communication and positive remarks could have optimized the situation and helped keep the system running smoothly.

The church is a spiritual formation system that is filled with processes. We have worship processes, education processes, care-giving processes, administrative processes, organizational processes, and relationship processes. These are just a few interrelated processes that link together to form the system we call church. When all these processes clearly move us toward a common goal, the system is optimized. However, when the processes are not mutually supportive, the system is suboptimized.

When the work of any system is compartmentalized, the danger of suboptimization increases. In the church, the work of various committees often is conducted as if it has nothing to do with the work of other committees. The evangelism committee does its thing, while the worship committee does its thing.

Christian education plans for Sunday school; and stewardship plans an annual campaign; and the missions committee holds a supper to raise funds and awareness. Quite often, these committees compete for money, space, calendar time, and people. There is a total lack of awareness that each function of the church needs to be aligned with every other function for the system to work properly. **Alignment** occurs when everything moves through the system toward a common end. If the work of the Christian education committee is to educate Christians, the work of the worship committee is to inspire Christians, and the work of the evangelism committee is to win Christians, there is no real alignment. However, if the work of Christian education is to create experiences where people can encounter and come to know God, the work of the worship committee is to create experiences where people can encounter and come to know God, and the work of the evangelism committee. . ., well, you get the point. Alignment moves the entire organization toward its desired outcome. The interrelationship of every activity is honored and understood. There is no competition for resources when all processes within the system are aligned for optimization.

Flow

Within systems, there is movement. Inputs move through the various processes. They are transformed into outputs that become new inputs for other processes. In systems language, the way things move through a system is called **flow**. For our purposes, we shall describe four types of flow: directional flow, destination flow, pendulum flow, and spiral flow.

Directional flow is exactly what it says — things flow in one direction. Rivers, one-way streets, roller coasters, clocks, and gravity all move in one direction, unless acted on by some unusual force. Directional flow keeps things moving in an orderly, predictable fashion. Things continue in a linear, progressive manner.

Often directional flow leads to a set terminus. Then it becomes **destination flow**. Most production lines are destination flows, where finished products end the process. The Dead Sea is an example of destination flow, where everything moves into the sea, but nothing exits. In the church, many people view the Christian life as destination flow. Once they have taken vows of membership, they feel they have completed the journey.

Pendulum flow repeats the same action over and over. Swinging, going to work, doing laundry, and going to church on Sunday are examples of pendulum flow. Pendulum flow is highly predictable, but never leads to change or improvement.

Spiral flow embraces the best elements of the other three types of flow. Spiral flow moves repeatedly in an upward direction toward the destination of continuous improvement. Learning, fitness training, and faithfully practicing the means of grace are illustrations of spiral flow.

In the church, spiral flow is the goal. All our systems and processes for faith formation are aligned to yield ever-improving results.

Continuous Improvement

The biblical edict to "be perfect as God is perfect" makes continuous improvement imperative within the church. There is no standard of "good enough." The Christian life is not heading toward a destination. The Christian life is a journey. No matter how well we know God, how much we pray, how loving and caring we may be, there is always room for improvement. W. Edwards Deming, the father of TQM (Total Quality Management), showed worldwide manufacturing that there was room for improvement in every aspect of production. Deming distinguished between excellence and quality. Excellence gave companies an excuse to stop improving, but the pursuit of quality ensured that an organization would never rest, never be satisfied with good enough.

This lesson is critically important for The United Methodist Church in the new millennium. Every aspect of our ministry, no matter how good it might be, requires careful and thorough evaluation. The ways we conduct worship, welcome strangers, visit the sick, teach the Bible, host dinners, care for the dying, and live our lives can all be improved. What is required is a commitment to quality — a commitment to be better tomorrow than we are today.

This sets a whole new standard for what it means to be the church. We no longer speak in terms of giving answers and solving problems, but of being a community on the way. We journey together, practicing the means of grace, growing and learning and leading every step of the way. We don't ask, "Are we there yet?" but "Where do we go from here?" We offer a model of continuous growth, exploration, and improvement. We strive to serve people better than they have been served in the past. As we improve our relationships, our communication, our ways of working together, and our structures for ministry, we raise people's hopes and expectations. We set high standards that stretch people and challenge their development. The church becomes more than just another group or club. It becomes an example of quality in a world that too often settles for mediocrity. The more the church establishes itself as a center of quality, the better it reflects the character and nature of God and Jesus Christ. A commitment to quality and continuous improvement is a commitment to honor and glorify God in all that we say and do.

If we are to align all our activities and processes toward the optimization of our church as a system, we must be clear about what it is we have been created and called to do. The task before us must be clearly understood and shared. Only then can we create the appropriate system to be a new kind of church in the world. We must, first and foremost, know our mission and develop a vision for living that mission together.

Chapter Eight Questions

1. In what ways do we promote "quality" over "excellence" in the church? What are the quality ministries in your church?
2. How do you evaluate spiritual growth and maturity in your congregation? What are the specific qualitative measures that you use?
3. Where do you find the greatest alignment in the ministries you offer with your mission and purpose? Where are activities disconnected from the larger sense of purpose and mission?
4. If you could only offer one thing to equip people to live faithfully in the world, what would it be? Why?

Chapter Nine:
Core Values, Mission, and Vision

During the past decade, the church adopted a passion for drafting elaborate mission and vision statements. In some cases, these visioning and mission-clarifying processes have motivated congregations and conferences to new levels of excellence in ministry. Sadly, this is the exception, rather than the rule. The problem lies in the very nature of turning mission or vision into statements written on pieces of paper. True mission doesn't need to be written, because it is so central to the very existence of an organization. Everyone who participates in the life of the organization — whether it be a church, club, or business — is aware of what that organization is all about. If a group needs to write down its reason for existence, then perhaps it doesn't need to exist.

Likewise, vision, by definition, is picture and image, not words on a page. Even picture language only captures a snapshot of a vision rather than the vision itself. Vision isn't something we create, but something we glimpse if we keep our eyes and hearts open. Giving a team a task of creating a vision is similar to giving the same group the task of making sure it is sunny on Thursday. Vision is God's gift, and every person perceives it differently.

Perhaps the clearest indication that mission- and vision-statement development processes are ineffectual is the number of times that such statements are set aside or forgotten shortly after they have generated a lot of activity and energy. Conflicts still arise, results are still less than stellar, and people still burn out and get frustrated. Clarifying mission and vision, while critically important, is only one step in a much larger systemic process.

Most annual conferences and local congregations begin their visioning and mission-clarification processes by making a wrong assumption. They assume that everyone involved shares the same core values and beliefs. After all, this is the church. It makes sense that people in the church would hold similar beliefs, values, and desires. Or does it? The values that form the foundation of each individual shape his or her attitudes, beliefs, practices, and dreams for the future.

Collectively, these values are reflected in the way we live, and they dramatically affect our understanding of the mission of the church and our vision for how the church might live most faithfully.

Values

What are the fundamental values upon which The United Methodist Church is founded? Be careful. Values are not what we do. They are not even limited to what we believe. Values explain why we believe what we believe and do what we do. I worship because I believe it is the right thing to do. Why do I believe this? Because I want to have a good relationship with God. Why? Because I believe that my life will be better if I have a relationship with God. Why? Because I want my life to be good and full and meaningful. My core values — a desire for life to be good and full and meaningful — drive my behavior. I shape my beliefs, attitudes, and practices around them. They are deeply personal; but not surprisingly, my values are shared by many other people. Conversely, many values that I assume are shared by all are unique to me and perhaps a few others, and herein lies the problem. Most of our conflicts within the church that we ascribe to difference of opinion or lack of understanding of the mission or vision of the church are actually differences in our fundamental values.

Although I spend a great deal of time talking about how I behave and what I believe, I rarely enter into a discussion about my values. Yet my core values lay the foundation upon which my life is built. This is true of our churches as well. Our mission — our sense of purpose — and our vision — the way we will live out our mission — are founded upon the core values of the members of the community of faith. Churches engage in elaborate processes for determining mission and vision, but few spend time reflecting on their core values.

Ezra Earl Jones describes the relationship between mission and vision by drawing a picture frame.[6] Mission is the frame, the parameters that describe who we are and what we do.

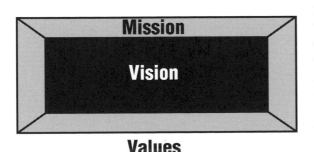

The vision is the picture for ministry contained within the frame of mission. Extending this image, core values are the wall upon which the frame is hung. The extent to which people will commit themselves to the pursuit of the mission and vision of the organization depends upon the extent to which the mission and vision represent their personal core values.

Traditionally, core values have not been discussed openly in the church. Usually, the exploration gets bogged down in deciding which values are "right" and which are inappropriate. Values clarification gives way to values prioritization. Communities influence and shape people's values, but this is a long, slow process. It is much more profitable to be aware of the values that are present than to attempt to create a core of acceptable shared values to which everyone must subscribe. The former meets people where they are; the latter presumes to judge that people should be elsewhere. It is enough to understand that all people hold values that determine who they are and what they believe. When individuals enter into community, there is a mixing and blending of different values. Some merge gracefully, some collide. All inform the way we relate to our community of faith. How is it possible to create a church that is meaningful and effective if we are ignorant of the values that motivate its members? How can we align all our energy and resources toward the fulfillment of our mission, if the mission has nothing to do with the values of the community? And if the vision for our community of faith emerges from the hearts of the people, understanding the core values is the only way we can understand the vision.

The Appendix contains a simple values exercise for use within local congregations, conference committees, and cabinets. It is an open-ended process that allows dialogue to begin identifying values without digressing into arguments about the "proper" values for Christians. Small groups across the country have responded to this exercise in three distinct ways:

1. It is the first opportunity they have had to talk about values in their congregation.
2. It helps them find common ground around which they do the work that they do.
3. It helps them understand that many of the problems they encounter working together are not due to misunderstandings or miscommunications, but to significant differences in personal values.

Said one district superintendent, "Focusing on values gives me the language I've been searching for to explain why our mission is our mission. It moves us from the 'what' to the 'why.'"

Mission

The 1996 session of the General Conference defined the mission of The United Methodist Church as "making disciples of Jesus Christ." This scriptural phrase helps define the "what" of the church — our purpose as an institution. It provides the frame within which each annual conference and each local congregation paints its picture for ministry. Defining and clearly understanding the mission of an organization is key to that organization's success.

Our mission, to make disciples of Jesus Christ, raises as many questions as it answers. What is a disciple? How is one made? How do you know when you have completed a disciple? Who is Jesus Christ? What does a disciple do once he or she is made? What is the ongoing responsibility of the church to disciples? All these questions provide a rich field of inquiry for the redefinition of our church in the new paradigm. Faith-forming communities will answer these questions very differently from congregations and conferences remaining in the activity-center paradigm.

The primary task of the church provides the framework for fulfilling our disciple-making mission.

We make disciples by reaching out and receiving people in the name of Jesus Christ, relating them to God, nurturing and strengthening them in their faith journeys, and sending them into the world to live transformed and transforming lives. This core process has not changed even though the paradigm has shifted. Churches in the activity-center paradigm fulfilled the primary task through programs and events. An evangelism committee took responsibility for reaching out and receiving. Worship committees designed services to relate people to God. Christian education and membership committees created opportunities for people to be nurtured and strengthened in their faith. Missions committees encouraged involvement in the world, either through active service or the giving of money and other aid. Each of these activities contributed to the overall primary task and the successful fulfillment of the mission of the church.

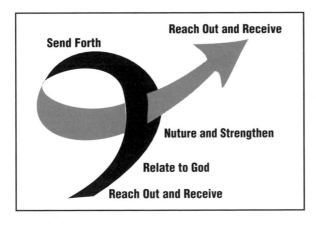

There is a fundamental flaw to approaching the mission of the church in this compartmentalized way. It ignores how the activities in our churches are connected to one another. It takes the work of the organization of the church and breaks it into component parts, ignoring the whole. The faith-forming-community paradigm begins by looking at the mission of the church — and more specifically at the primary task — as a system; and it pays more attention to the way all the parts work together than to the parts themselves. Each activity, process, and program of a church must align with its mission. Each phase of the primary task is present in all work of the church. Evangelism is a process of reaching out and receiving, relating to God, nurturing and strengthening, and then sending forth. The same is true of Christian education, stewardship, worship, missions, and so on. Everything we do is connected to everything else we do; and it reflects the core process, the primary task, of the church. If an activity does not align with the primary task, then we should not be doing it.

The mission of the church describes clearly why we exist. It is not open to debate. If we disagree with the mission, then we need to find another church or organization. The mission defines the organization, and people come together to support and fulfill that mission. The words we use might vary from place to place, but the intention is the same. Making disciples of Jesus Christ is the mission that defines United Methodism. We balance the upbuilding and support of Christian community within so that we might live differently in the world. We do not ask, "Do we agree with this mission?" but, "How can we best fulfill this mission?" The way we answer this question in each local setting — whether it be at the national, annual conference, or congregational level — is our vision.

Vision

A decade ago, we spoke of vision as something "out there" in the future. Early proponents of vision talked about identifying our current reality and looking into the future to find out where we need to go. That destination was our vision.

Today, systems thinking has transformed the visioning process. Now we speak in terms of identifying current reality, desired reality, and the paths or bridges that move us from where we are to where we need to go. The entire picture is the vision.

Current reality is where we are today. Identifying current reality requires that we understand the people who make up the organization, what they think and believe, what their passions are, where they come from, and where they hope to go in the future. Current reality includes the practices, rituals, and traditions of the community of faith. It includes the cultural and community context in which the community of faith is located. Current reality changes every day, so identifying it is a monitoring process, not a one-time event. A clear understanding of current reality helps us grasp the human and material resources that make up the church at any given time. It charts our location on the map and identifies our starting point.

Desired reality is the hopes, dreams, passions, and plans of the community of faith for the future. Some parts may reflect the immediate future, while other parts may be far away. Some aspects of the desired reality are quite clear and well-understood, while others are fuzzy and somewhat confusing. Various people see different things when they view the desired reality. Perhaps "desired realities" is a more accurate term. What defines the appropriateness of the desired reality is whether it fits the frame of the mission and aligns with the primary task.

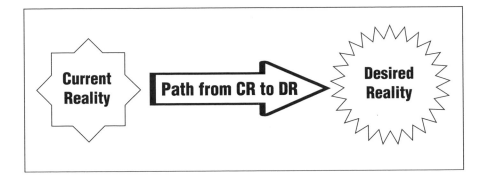

However, just casting a picture of the future is inadequate to create a vision for the group. Unless the vision includes the means for moving from the current reality to the desired reality, it becomes demoralizing and fails to motivate people to action. Although not every step in the process is clear, the leaders continue to point the way and lay out the steps. Great visionaries throughout the ages have admitted that they do not always know all the answers, but say that they gained greater clarity about the right steps to take and the best decisions to make along the way.

The clearer that current reality, desired reality, and the paths from one to the other are defined, the better able people are to "get it." Change creates tension, and people need to understand what is happening to them and why. Most people are satisfied with current reality. Moving to a new reality is always threatening to some people. The more that the new territory can be charted, the more comfortable people will be to make the journey.

There is one more vitally important thing to keep in mind — the path from current reality to desired reality is not a simple move from one point to another. When we talk about current reality, we are talking about one position along a pre-existing trajectory. Our congregations are already heading somewhere. If we do absolutely nothing, we will still move forward into the future. It is as important to understand where we are currently heading as it is to know where God wants us to be. The current trajectory of a congregation exerts an incredible amount of inertia — any time we try to move in a new direction, all the power of the status quo fights to hold us in place. We need to understand the forces that pull us back — resistance to change, fear, comfort, tradition, security, caution, etc. — in order to counteract inertia. While it may appear that people are resisting growth and progress, in reality they are fighting to preserve the familiar. To lead a community toward a new vision requires that we not only learn and do new things, but that we "unlearn" and stop doing some old things.

Margaret Wheatley, author of *Leadership and the New Science* and *A Simpler Way*, offers a helpful model to summarize the importance of the entire visioning process.[7]

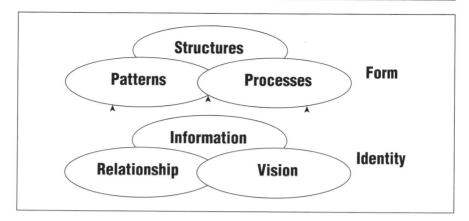

Wheatley says that when organizations begin to talk about change, they ordinarily focus on altering their structures, patterns, or processes — the form the organization takes. They decide to "do" things differently. However, modifying behavior is no guarantee of radical, fundamental, systemic change. Instead, real change occurs at the deeper level — the level of our identity. The information we share identifies who we are. Our relationships — the way we work together and combine to create synergy — identify our potential. Our vision — the hopes, dreams, desires, and plans that motivate and inspire us — points us in the direction we most want to go. When we spend our time reflecting on the deeper issues, changes in structures, patterns, and processes automatically happen. It is at the level of identity — information, relationships, and vision — that the mission, vision, and values processes come into play in the church. When we engage in these processes with integrity, the bridges and paths   structures, processes, and patterns   emerge, and we are empowered to be a new kind of church. Transformation is what the church is all about. Through the crucial work of mission, vision, and values clarification, we attain the renewal and revitalization we so deeply desire.

The key to developing a systems approach to our ministry that begins building on the foundation of values, mission, and vision is leadership. The grand scope of the visioning process requires that we free leaders to lead instead of to manage what is already in place. It is to a different kind of leadership that we now turn our attention.

Chapter Nine Questions

1. What are the core values shared by the majority of the congregation?
2. How are these values reflected and revealed through the ministries and practices of the congregation?
3. In what ways do the leaders and participants of your congregation attend to and discern God's will for the church?
4. What are the strengths and assets from which you draw to move toward a better future?
5. What are the forces of inertia that hold you in place and fight against changes and new directions?

Chapter Ten:
Learning Leaders

One simple truth is that a new kind of church will require a brand new kind of leadership. The old models of hierarchical, top-down, single-person-in-charge leadership will be less and less effective the further we move into the emerging paradigm. It is questionable whether these models of leadership were ever appropriate for the church. While Paul and Jesus both modeled leadership in these ways, the context in which they led was quite different; and a strong case can be made that most leaders today are not modern-day versions of Jesus or Paul.

For a generation or more, The United Methodist Church has borrowed its leadership models from the secular world. There is nothing wrong with assimilating helpful practices and principles; however, one danger of borrowing is that the essential core of the institution may get lost. One critical distinction that needs to be made is that the church fundamentally requires spiritual leadership. Spiritual leadership is of a whole different breed than what is normally described in the secular culture as "effective leadership." Compare the two lists below.

LEADERS	SPIRITUAL LEADERS
Integrity	Integrity
Authority	Spiritual center
Knowledge	Vision
Vision	Honesty
Decision-making ability	Fairness
Charisma	Knowledge
Command of language	Patience
Shrewdness	Wisdom
Courage	Teaching ability

These are the key characteristics of "leaders" and "spiritual leaders" as reported by various groups in seminars held across the country.[8]

What similarities and differences do you notice? Most of the literature being published on leadership deals with the list on the left. As the church moves fully into the new paradigm, the focus will shift to the list on the right.

In the business world, as in the church, integrity is the most highly prized attribute of leadership. Leaders who "walk the talk" — who are consistent in the ways they talk and act — are viewed as the best kind of leaders. But the supporting qualities of leadership are vastly different in the two spheres. As one workshop participant noted, the supporting characteristics of the secular leader have to do with power and skill. The supporting qualities of the spiritual leader have to do with character and substance. While this distinction might be too simplistic, it gets at the heart of the issue for the church in the twenty-first century: people expect leadership in the church to be different from leadership in the world. As you read through the qualities of effective spiritual leaders, think in terms of both clergy and laity.

Integrity

Who comes to mind when you hear the word "integrity"? There was a time when pastors ranked near the top of any such list. Is that still true today? Although pastors may be ahead of politicians and lawyers on the list (in some cases), simply being an ordained leader affords no special reward where integrity is concerned. Too many church leaders have failed to "practice what they preach," and many people are skeptical.

Integrity is a commitment to doing what is right, honest, and good. Integrity is earned through consistency and trustworthiness. A leader's integrity is under continuous scrutiny. It may take years to build integrity, but it can be brought toppling down in an instant.

Integrity is more than doing the right things for the right reasons. When people are asked to explain what they mean by integrity, they talk about leaders who live a life centered in the values and principles that they teach. They "integrate" what they say and what they do in a meaningful way that provides a model for living. Many people look to their Christian leaders to exemplify what it means to be Christian. Some will say that this is unfair and unrealistic, but it is the current reality nonetheless. Integrity is consistency in thought, word, and action.

Spiritual Centering

What makes a Christian different from a non-Christian? Christians are just people, but there are marks that signal a differentiation. Christian beliefs and spiritual practices influence the way a Christian lives. For United Methodists, John Wesley offered specific instruction to participate in the means of grace —

prayer, celebration of the Lord's Supper, study of the Scriptures, fasting, acts of mercy, Christian conference — which focus the Christian upon God. When a Christian leader practices the means of grace, he or she offers a model for a different kind of leadership. Confidence in a spiritual leader blossoms when the leader's devotional life is evident. Not only is confidence inspired, but valuable teaching occurs. In the church, people are looking for leaders who pray regularly, know the Bible, teach spiritual discipline, and are comfortable talking about matters of faith. The spiritually centered leader feels free to bring God into any discussion, and he or she helps remind followers that God's will matters in the decision-making processes we employ.

Vision

People report that vision is one of the greatest confidence builders in those who claim to lead. One man at a recent seminar commented that he had the utmost confidence in his pastor, a woman who had brought about great change in his church. "She always seems to know exactly where she wants to go. She listens to our hopes, dreams, and fears, and then offers a wonderful picture for how we might live into the future. It is simply amazing!"

It is not always important that leaders generate the vision, but it is essential that those in leadership be able to clearly articulate the vision and hold the organization on course toward the vision. Visionary leaders are those who see beyond the constraints of current reality to something new, something larger, something better.

Honesty

For leadership in the church, honesty appears to be an obvious quality. However, the media have exposed numerous "moral and ethical" leaders to be adept at telling fibs, fabrications, and half-truths. Honesty is no longer listed among the top attributes of secular leaders, but it is very important to members of our churches. People in the church want to be able to trust and believe in the teachings and counsel of Christian leaders. Speaking the truth in love is a biblical admonition that helps set the church apart from other institutions. Where honesty prevails, trust is built; and the church models a better way for people to relate to one another.

Fairness

In a turbulent world, people are seeking comfort, balance, and justice. They want to be treated with fairness and respect. In our congregations, where so many people feel insignificant and of little self worth, it is important to treat everyone equally. Inclusive language is an appeal by women and ethnic groups to be treated with the same measure of care and respect as anyone else. People are looking for places where they can be affirmed for who they are, where they won't be discriminated against, and where they will be honored as valuable human beings. The church stands in a unique position to offer such a place, and it will exist where leaders are committed to fairness and justice.

Knowledge

Spiritual leaders have a deep knowledge of the Bible, the beliefs and practices of the people, and ways to apply spiritual truths to everyday life. Leaders of local congregations make the commitment to improve their knowledge continuously, not only of the Bible and theology, but of the world in which they live. People will look to spiritual leaders to tell them not only what the Bible says, but also to help them understand what it means. Reading, studying, training, and learning are all part of a leader's ongoing development. The best learners are teachers, and they share what they learn with others. People respect knowledgeable, competent leaders. Leadership for the twenty-first century will require a dedication to continuous learning.

Patience

A young executive from Delaware contrasted leadership where he worked with the leadership in his church. "At work, we're told to get with the program or get left behind. At church, our pastor says, 'We're all in this together.' The difference is that the church is focused on how to help me, whereas my business is always looking at how I can help it."

Patience is an essential quality for church leaders. People want to be helped through change. They want adequate space in which to learn. In a world that perpetually places pressure upon them, many people seek solace from the storm. They want the church to give them grace, not stress. Leaders create the environment for growth and development, and patience is the key to helping people relax into growth and development. Where leaders are patient, growing disciples flourish.

Wisdom

Western culture does not put great stock in wisdom. Knowledge, information, facts, and figures tend to carry more weight in most people's minds. But in the church, people are hungry for practical tools and information to help them make sense of their faith and of their lives. Listening to leaders who exhibit keen insight and common sense instills confidence and builds trust. In the new paradigm, people no longer listen to a leader because of his or her position. They listen because the leader has earned the right to be heard. In conversations about the qualities of spiritual leaders, people say that wisdom is second only to integrity in determining the level of respect they have for a leader.

Teaching Ability

Knowledge, wisdom, and vision are all essential for spiritual leadership; but without the ability to communicate effectively, none of the other qualities make much difference. As our culture becomes more sophisticated in its ability to communicate, so leaders in the church must match this sophistication to teach and model Christian living.

Teaching is a gift, but it is also a talent that can be learned, developed, and improved. As we move into the new paradigm, where the church will grow as a learning organization, teaching and learning will go hand in hand. It has been shown by many educators that the best way to learn is to teach. Leaders who teach are the best learners; those who constantly learn have the most to teach. Learning-teaching leaders create environments where real learning can take place by all. Modeling the dynamic relationship between teaching and learning is one of the most critical qualities of spiritual leadership.

Each of these qualities is related to every other quality. Secular writings about leadership rarely examine issues of wisdom, patience, fairness, and teaching ability. Only when we shift the focus to spiritual leadership do these characteristics emerge. Taken as a whole, the nine characteristics of spiritual leadership are exemplified by the life and ministry of Jesus Christ. Every one of the qualities of the spiritual leader can be illustrated in the gospels.

The Changing Nature of Leadership

Having examined the qualities of spiritual leadership, it is important to turn attention to the shifting nature of leadership. Spiritual leaders lead in a new way in the new paradigm.

The most profound change in leadership for a new kind of church is that it is team-based rather than solo leadership. In the old paradigm, one person could conceivably lead an entire congregation. In the fast-paced change and diversity of the postmodern church, the leadership task is larger than any one person, regardless of his or her gifts and abilities. A single individual may assume the position of "the leader," but leadership is best a shared activity. One way of understanding the shift is to think about the pastor as shepherd. In the old paradigm, the pastor was the shepherd of a flock of sheep — all similar, all moderately docile. In the new paradigm, pastoring a congregation more nearly resembles shepherding a zoo where all the bars have been removed. The job is too massive and too complex for one person.

Sharing power and responsibility is a new idea for many leaders. The cultural models of leadership predominantly elevate the skills and abilities of the individual. Effective leaders are "new messiahs" who deliver us to the promised land. We respect those people who can perform Herculean feats and give the impression of being invincible. The rare individual does appear who has the charisma, ability, and drive to go it alone; but ultimately such individuals make it more difficult for the rest of us. Too few people are born leaders, with all the equipment intact. For the vast majority, we need to learn as we go how to be more effective as leaders. The journey is lonely and fraught with peril when we go it alone. Team leadership allows individuals to contribute what they have to offer without the burden of having to be good at everything. Together, leadership becomes an exercise in synergy. Synergy exists when the total is greater than the sum of the parts. The key determinant of effective leadership in the new paradigm, both in business and in the church, will be synergy.

Another significant shift in the nature of leadership is one of communication. In the past, leaders told followers what they needed to know, what they needed to do, and where they needed to go. The emphasis today is shifting away from telling to asking — then listening.

Listening is the most vital leadership skill needing development as we move into the new paradigm. Hearing the deepest needs and yearnings of people gives rise to the best ways to serve, to lead, to teach, and to build relationships. We can empower people only as we come to know their areas of disempowerment. We can offer healing to people only after we have listened to learn where they hurt.

Listening leaders do not start from a position of having all the answers. Instead, these leaders invite followers to join them in a journey of exploration to discover new ideas and information that can yield the answers and solutions people seek. A primary work of leaders in the new paradigm will be learning.

Learning leaders are growing leaders who model what it means to be Christian in a chaotic world. Learning produces flexibility, and flexibility makes us "change ready." True learning occurs best in group settings where individuals are allowed to learn and teach and be in dialogue around the ideas they encounter. The computer generation has taught us that interactive learning is the most effective style of learning. With the massive amount of information and data available in today's technological society, a commitment to learning is not an option for effective leaders; it is imperative.

The Changing Role of Leadership

As we move from the activity-center paradigm, where the ministries of the church are performed by hired staff and a select core of volunteers, to the faith-forming-community paradigm, where all members of the fellowship are involved in meaningful service, a significantly different style of leadership is necessary. The role of paid professional leaders is to fulfill the demands of a job description. The role of a minister of the gospel of Jesus Christ, whether ordained or lay, is to fulfill the call and to serve effectively from the gifts God gives. Leadership in the faith-forming-community paradigm will create an environment where every person can find a place for learning, growth, formation, and meaningful service.

To accomplish this shift into the new paradigm, leaders of The United Methodist Church — at all levels — will need to focus attention in four areas: (1) to accurately identify the current reality of the church, (2) to articulate the desired reality of the people, (3) to design appropriate systems to move the church from its current reality to its desired reality, and (4) to adopt a "balcony perspective" to observe and improve the entire process.[9]

Name Current Reality

Leaders in the church must assume responsibility for making sure that everyone fully understands current reality — where we are, how we got here, who we are at this moment in time, and what human and material resources we have. This is the most critical phase in any visioning process. Too often, leaders assume that the current reality is fully understood; hence, too little time is given to identifying the way things really are.

Current reality is not identified once for all time. If our church is moving, growing, changing, and learning, then our current reality will evolve. Just as a navigator monitors progress, watches the gauges, charts, and terrain; so leaders in the new paradigm will need to adopt the navigator function for the church. Leaders will be able to say with confidence to anyone who asks, "This is where we are."

Articulate the Desired Reality

Likewise, leaders in the faith-forming-community paradigm must be able to state with equal confidence, "This is where we are going." Remember, it is not necessary for leaders to generate the desired reality. If they have listened to the deepest desires of the people and if they have clarity about the mission of the church, they are able to articulate and clarify the vision of desired reality so that it is understood by all.

As with current reality, desired reality is not static. As we grow, and as we move closer to our desired reality, new visions for the future will arise. We will see new possibilities, new ways to serve God and neighbor in the world. What excites and motivates us in our journey at one point may be completely different at another point. To articulate the desired reality requires continuous listening to all the people on the journey. When desired reality is a constant topic of conversation, it becomes almost impossible to get "stuck." Leaders move the church forward by perpetually lifting up a compelling vision for the future.

Designing Appropriate Systems

Knowing where we are and where we want to go are both essential processes, but they are meaningless without a clear sense of how to get from one to the other. A critical function of leadership in the new paradigm is that of cartographer — drawing the maps that will allow us to travel from current reality to desired reality. Remember the illustration of the visioning process on page 71. A vision is incomplete when it identifies only the starting point and the destination. It must also illustrate how we can achieve the fulfillment of our mission.

The tendency in the activity-center model of the church is to begin with our systems already in place, then to accomplish only that which the extant system allows. This greatly limits the potential of the church. People should not serve the structures; the structures should serve the people.

The activity-center paradigm is structure based. In many cases, the structure

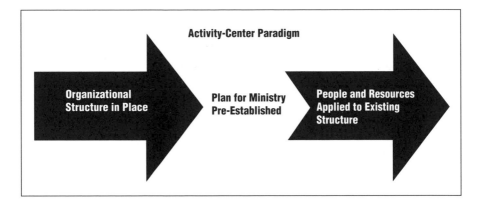

Activity-Center Paradigm

Organizational Structure in Place

Plan for Ministry Pre-Established

People and Resources Applied to Existing Structure

was determined by a former generation of leaders and has been perpetuated through numerous changes in leadership with a "we've-always-done-it-this-way" mentality. Over the years, the ministries and programs of a conference or local church have been established out of the existing structure and have been institutionalized. Then, with both structure and program in place, an endless stream of clergy and laity are processed through the system. In such a system, there is little opportunity to determine if the structure and program are appropriate. The only things changed are the people.

In the faith-forming-community paradigm, however, the focus is not primarily on structure, but on people. When the focus is on people, the potential is almost limitless. Whole new vistas open up for the work and ministry we can perform.

A gifts-based, people-oriented system is not common in The United Methodist Church today. It will require leaders with a commitment to create a new kind of church to make the transformation happen. This process is a full-time, comprehensive, and consuming job. Other functions of organization, administration, design, and implementation will need to be handled by other ministers in the conferences and congregations. The role of leadership is to make sure that the church organizes for ministry in such a way that people may live fully into the faith-forming-community paradigm. We no longer have the luxury of merely managing the existing structures and calling

Faith-Forming-Community Paradigm

Gifts, Passions, and Resources of the People Assessed (Current Reality)

Hopes, Plans, Dreams Emerge on the Journey (Desired Reality)

Appropriate Systems Designed to Move from Current Reality to Desired Reality

it leadership. The time has come (indeed it is past) when we must be clear about the difference between management and leadership.

The Balcony Perspective

Watching a play or a movie from the orchestra level is a completely different experience from watching it from the balcony. Although the orchestra level places the viewer close to — if not in the middle of — the action, it allows the person to watch only a portion of the action at any one time. Being so close to the performance makes it difficult to attend to the "big picture" — all the action and activity that occurs on other portions of the stage or screen.

The balcony affords an entirely different view. From the perspective of distance and height, the viewer can take in the entire scene. Details missed up close emerge from a distance. Interaction and interrelationships become clear. The balcony perspective offers a systems view.

Leaders need to be able to see the entire system. Continuous improvement depends on being able to monitor all the processes in a system. Not only is identifying the parts important, but seeing how the parts fit and work together is essential. When leaders are constantly caught up in "doing" the administrative and program work of the church, they have little time to take the "balcony perspective." Without the balcony perspective, leaders cannot accurately assess and evaluate the appropriateness of the system for moving from current reality to desired reality.

Perhaps the most daunting task facing leaders in the faith-forming-community paradigm is to design systems for ministry that allow leaders to lead. We are slowly emerging from a period where we believed that everyone was a leader. Not everyone wants to lead. Not everyone is gifted to lead. Not everyone has the skills and graces to lead. This does not mean that those people have nothing of value to contribute to the leadership of the church. The new paradigm is offering wonderful images of leaders and followers in a partnership that resembles a dance more than a parade.

Common sense tells us that without followers, there is no need for leaders. Without disciples, there is no need for teachers. Without pilgrims, there is no need for guides. Leadership is a special and specialized role within the church. For too long, we have defined leaders as those who are hired, appointed, and elected to do the work of the church. Leaders lead the entire community in accomplishing the work of Christ. Anything less is not leadership.

Reclaiming the Laos

There is great confusion in the church over the relationship between the clergy and the laity, especially when it comes to leadership within the church. Most biblical scholars agree that there is no clear distinction between clergy and laity in the New Testament. The division, the notion that clergy are somehow set apart from or set above the laity, developed by medieval times; and it has prevailed since. This division is unfortunate, since our Scriptures — both Old and New Testament — clearly define the common call, vocation, and priesthood shared by the whole people of God (the Laos). Ordination, once a sign of special responsibility and accountability, devolved into a confirmation of authority and power. Lay ministry was degraded, while the ministry of the clergy was elevated. The current popularity of the phrase "empowerment of the laity" should raise the question, "How did the laity lose power in the first place?"

The New Testament, particularly the writings in the name of the Apostle Paul, provides an image of the church as the body of Christ, defined as and composed of gifted men and women, knit together to continue the work begun by Jesus of Nazareth. It is quite clear that Christ is the head of the body, not a pastor. Ordained clergy leaders are one part of the body, just as everyone else. The church is clergy and laity joined together by gifts, graces, and the love of God to carry Christ into the world. No one person is more essential to that work than any other.

Aileen Williams, a layperson from the Minnesota Annual Conference, offers the most helpful distinction for the new paradigm when she describes leaders in terms of "appointed" and "resident" leaders. In our itinerant system, some leaders move from place to place, while others stay within a community for the long term. Appointed leaders are sent into conference and congregational systems to bring their gifts and skills to bear on the needs of the community of faith. Resident leaders fundamentally define the character and identity of the community of faith. The gifts and service that they provide to the organization are of no less importance or impact than those of the appointed leaders.

Leaders, both lay and clergy, who will move the church into the faith-forming-community paradigm are willing to let go of power, prestige, and territory so that the mission of the church and the will of God might be accomplished. Personal agendas and inflated egos get set aside as the good of the community takes center stage.

On a trip to the northeast, I encountered a pastor who told me about all the exciting books she had read and all the wonderful movies she had seen. Knowing that this woman is the pastor of a thriving church and that she is no slacker, I inquired how she found the time to read so much and go to the movies so often. She laughed and said, "I spent the first twenty years of my ministry doing everything myself. I preached, I led worship, I taught, I counseled, I visited, I wrote letters, I led meetings — then, one day, it hit me. I'm working too hard! And I'm not getting the results I really want. I'm not leading. I'm managing.

"I decided then and there that the only way I could work less was to get other people to work more. Instead of teaching, I taught others to teach. Instead of preaching, I taught others to preach. I taught them to visit. I taught them to counsel. I taught them to manage.

"Looking back, I realize that I was a pastor in the worst sense of the word — I was treating people like sheep. Instead, I started treating them like disciples. Disciples can become teachers; sheep can't become shepherds.

"Now I have a church full of people who are preaching, teaching, and healing. And me? I watch, and read, and think, and listen. And you know what? I'm a much better pastor today than I was when I was doing everything myself."

This is the pastor of the new paradigm — someone who uses her skills and gifts to lead others who will lead others. She does not see herself as being "in charge" of her church, but as being "in partnership" with the church. This refreshing understanding of leadership is the key to an effective shift from the activity-center paradigm to the faith-forming-community paradigm.

Chapter Ten Questions

1. Reflect on the two leadership lists. What do you believe are the most important differences between secular and spiritual leaders?

2. As a group exercise, write each of the characteristics of a good spiritual leader on an index card or Post-It® Note. In groups of three to five, prioritize them from most important to lesser importance. Pay as much attention to the process of deciding as your final results. Compare lists.

3. Compare the relative strengths and weaknesses of the structure-based Activity-Center church and the gifts-based Faith Forming Community church. What hurdles must your congregation clear to move from a structure-based church to a gifts-based church? (If you have already made the shift, what were the greatest challenges you encountered?)

4. How well do the participants in the church understand themselves as leaders and ministers? How well do the leaders in the congregation share power and authority? Where does it work well? Where are the greatest opportunities for improvement?

Chapter Eleven:
Breaking Free

In the blockbuster film *Armageddon*, an asteroid is hurtling through space toward earth, threatening to wipe out all life on the planet. The only way to divert the destructive force is through external intervention — teams of astronauts and oil-rig drillers sent to plant nuclear devices inside the behemoth to blow it apart. The asteroid's momentum and trajectory were set, and its inertia made the asteroid highly resistant to change.

It may be an overstatement to compare the activity-center paradigm to a life-threatening asteroid; but without intervention, change is not likely. Inertia, the resistance to change and the tendency of an object to follow a prescribed trajectory, may be the most destructive force at work in the church today. As strongly as we might wish to defend the existent structure of Methodism, the truth is that The United Methodist Church is on a trajectory of steady decline and diminishing resources.

This chapter explores some of the forces that are necessary to intervene in our situation to move us into the new paradigm. Obviously, systems thinking; clarity of mission, vision, and values; and effective leadership are critical factors. In addition, moving the church into the new paradigm will require a radical reorientation in three areas: building relationships, sharing information, and managing change.

The word "orientation" originally meant "to turn toward the east." Travelers by both land and sea could gain their bearings each dawn by watching where the sun came up, and they could travel at night by following stars as they crested the horizon. Three such travelers "oriented" themselves to visit the baby Jesus in Bethlehem. Disorientation was to be lost, to lose sight of the markers and signs that made for a successful journey.

The business of the church is to make disciples of Jesus Christ. This is the journey. Currently, we are disoriented — not sure which direction to go to reach our objective. Reorienting ourselves will require turning around. Interestingly, the word "sin" means, "to miss the mark." The word "repentance" means, "To turn back toward the mark." The church stands at a critical repentance point. Now is the time to get oriented so that we might effectively achieve God's purposes in the world.

Building Relationships

In two large-group settings — one in Iowa, one in Southern California — participants were asked, "Why do you go to church?" Out of a wide range of answers, two very interesting tendencies occurred. One group said that they went to church to feel close to God. When they were in church, they wanted to be left alone. They wanted to sit in silence, listen for God, participate in worship or study, then go home. They didn't come for talk or fellowship, but for a personal and private experience of God.

The other group stated that they came seeking community and connection. They were looking for a deeply spiritual connection, but not with God alone. For many, it was important that they find a group of like-minded people with whom they could share and discuss their faith. They wanted to be active in experiences beyond worship and study. They wanted to work and play with other Christian people. Connection was foremost in their desire for being in the church.

These answers occupy opposite ends of the spectrum, but they point out to us — in both positive and negative ways — the need for relationship building in the church. Private pietism is a recent development in the whole of church history. Both Old and New Testaments and the doctrine and practice of the first eighteen centuries of the Christian church illustrate the communal nature of the church. We are a people of God. It is in community and communion that we become Christian disciples. Personal, private practices of devotion and spiritual formation are important, but they are not enough. It is in relationship that synergy occurs. It is in linking our gifts, our thoughts, our beliefs, and our practices with others that we form the body of Christ.

The challenge for the church is to examine our current activities and ask, "Are these experiences helping or hindering our process of relationship building?" If we merely allow people to enter into the church building without entering into community, we fail to fulfill the primary task of the church, thereby failing our mission. Certainly, individuals need nurture and feeding, but they need more than that. The church is defined by the interrelationship of its members.

On the other hand, what we have defined as fellowship for the past few generations — getting together socially to eat and sing and play — cannot define the church. Our churches are more than social clubs for people's enjoyment: the church is the incarnate body of Christ, representing to the world who God and Jesus Christ are. The church is about more than our desire for connection with others.

A necessary third element for the church today is our communal relationship with God. Our individual desire to know God and our desire to be connected to other people are both secondary to our need to know and do God's will as a people of God. Church participation — as defined in the faith-forming-community paradigm — is God's idea as revealed in Jesus Christ. Together, we are the church. Together, we are the body of Christ. Together, we have the power to transform the world.

The transformation of the world is the remaining essential element in moving the church into the new paradigm. The church is a unique institution in that it exists primarily for the benefit of its nonmembers, rather than for its members. The church exists to serve the world and to share the good news with those who have never heard it or who choose to ignore or resist it. Regardless of the response of the people outside the institution of the church, the church still holds a responsibility to love, care for, heal, and serve those people.

Even churches firmly rooted in the activity-center model can begin to break free of the limiting and exhausting business of their existing structures. Any activity in which we engage that does not allow us to build and strengthen relationships with God and Christian community is an activity we should cease. Anything we do that does not align with our primary task of reaching out and receiving people in the name of Christ, relating people to God, nurturing and strengthening people in their faith, and then sending them back into the world to live transformed and transforming lives is a waste of time, energy, and resources. This may sound harsh, but the current reality in our world means that we have only so much time and so much energy and so much money with which to work. We may be leaving a period of needing-doing for a time of having-being, but this doesn't mean that we actually have more to work with — just that we have a much healthier view of what we actually possess. The time has come for the church to regain focus and clarity about what it can do. This is the essence of vision.

A layperson from a church in Arkansas told me that she quit her board of trustees because it voted to allow a garden club instead of a prayer group to meet at the church. The rationale given was that the garden club contributed $75 a month to the church; the prayer group gave nothing; and the garden club was better attended. This illustrates the type of focus we're talking about. Holding up the frame of our mission and seeing clearly a vision moves us closer to the fulfillment of our primary task. Anything outside that frame is not what we're about — even when it does help build relationships. In the same way that there is a difference between secular and spiritual leadership, there is a difference between forming community and forming spiritual community. Our relationship building is always of a triangular nature — between me, you, and God.

Sharing Information

Information is power. The more deeply we move into an information-based society, the truer this will become. In the activity-center paradigm, information belonged in the hands of the few; and the channels along which information traveled were often narrow and few. Consequently, power rested in the hands of a few individuals, and disagreements arose through misunderstanding and confusion. Power plays would crop up as one group determined that it knew better than others what should happen. Financial records would be closed, so that only one or two individuals comprehended the accurate state of affairs, and decisions often got made through unofficial channels by those "in-the-know."

It is easy to see how this is a design for disaster. Since the system is designed for the results it is getting, an organization's system designed to empower the few will never grow to its full potential. The system for growth and health in the faith-forming-community paradigm is a system of continuous learning and free information sharing, where innovation, creativity, and pioneering are all valued and encouraged. As the new paradigm requires learning leaders, so too, it demands learning at all levels.

What would an environment of freedom and acceptance for new and different ideas look like? What happens to people's creativity and enthusiasm when the threat of punishment for failure is removed? How does it change an organization when the lowest-level member is respected and listened to with as much intensity as the most respected member? What happens when a group makes a commitment not to fear new ideas, different approaches to life, and change? These are the questions that lead us to reflect on the nature of the church in the faith-forming-community paradigm.

Each and every person offers a wealth of ideas, knowledge, skills, and creativity. When individuals are encouraged to link their life experience, training, and learning with that of others, amazing things can happen. The risk is that it is not always controllable. Give people a little freedom and encouragement, and they will change the world. At least, they will change the church. For some, this is a frightening and threatening thought. But, then, what about the existing church is so great that it cannot be improved? People love the church. People are excited about the church. People want the best for the church. Faith-forming communities trust people and call them to rise to the full potential of their God-giftedness.

The key to such a transformation is information. Everyone needs to have full access to the pertinent information in the church. Closed meetings, closed financial records, closed doors, and closed minds all lead to gossip, frustration, anger, and mistrust. What church can grow strong on such a foundation? As we move into the future, an atmosphere of mutual trust, respect, and open communication will prevail if we hope to grow.

A young man lamented that he had attempted to get involved with his local United Methodist congregation, but that it was impossible. "I really wanted to be active, and so I asked a lot of questions. It was a bad move on my part. I asked about why the minister was the only one who did certain things, and I was told not to worry about it. I asked how the money got spent, and they said it was none of my business. I read the *Book of Discipline* and asked why so many of the things our church did violated what the *Discipline* said, and I got the reputation of being a troublemaker. Before long, it was clear that I was no longer wanted there. I'm at a Congregational Church now, and it's like another planet. Everybody knows everything about everything!"

The United Methodist Church can not expect to survive long as a "secret society" where we have anything to hide. People are looking for honesty and integrity. We live in a seeker society where people have questions that they want answered. People are suspicious of those who act as if they have something to hide. If we hope to turn the trend around in our church, then we need to enter into dialogue with those who question. Communication in the activity-center paradigm tends to take the form of monologue, rather than dialogue. Sermons, a primary form of communication in the church, are predominantly one-way (with some racial-ethnic exceptions). Much information is communicated in letters, newsletters, bulletins, on posters and fliers, and other single direction media. It is easy to keep secrets and dispense only select information in one-way communication. Faith-forming communities will break free of one-way communication to enter into free-flowing dialogue.

One clear shift is already emerging. Worship long defined church participation in many people's minds. However, much of what occurs in worship is one way — prayers are preprinted and recited, Scriptures are read, anthems are sung, sermons are preached, and collection plates are brought to the congregation. What response is allowed is usually predesigned — responsive readings, doxologies, litanies, offerings — rather than spontaneous. Interaction is low, at best.

It was not always so. What characterized worship in the temple in Jesus' time was highly interactive; there was much questioning, debating, studying, and reflecting. Worship in the temple had much more in common with a lively Bible study than with a passive twentieth-century worship service. Of course, in Jesus' day the model wasn't perfect — women weren't allowed to participate in this provocative learning — but it challenges what we have allowed worship to become.

Many newcomers to the church are not finding their way into worship, but into small groups. Younger people tend to find worship impersonal and confusing. There is no freedom to raise questions or to say, "I don't understand." Small groups centered in Bible study, spiritual direction, and faith formation are much more appealing to seekers hungering for meaning. There is a great appeal in settings where exploration and journey can occur. A college senior characterized this difference when she said, "In worship, I get told by others who the church thinks I ought to be. In my small group, I get help finding out who God wants me to be." Is it any wonder that for this young woman and thousands like her a small group is her "church"? This is not to say that worship is an optional practice in the Christian faith, but that our definition of worship needs to be expanded. A large corporate gathering on Sunday morning is just one of many possible options. Our inability to accept alternative options for worship is one more indication that we need help dealing with change.

Managing Change

It is not change that people dislike, but being changed. When people have a sense of control over what is happening to them, when they can see clearly how change benefits them, and when they are secure in the knowledge that they will not lose anything, then (and only then) will they learn to embrace change. The church stands in a singular position to help people manage change. Faith in Jesus Christ and a spiritual centering in God offer the strongest support to move people fearlessly through the massive change all around them. As we grow together in faith-forming communities, we can develop networks of support and strength to enable one another to navigate the white-water rapids of change.

Understanding the nature of change is crucial. Essentially, change takes one of three forms — external change that happens to us and is beyond our control, natural internal change that happens to us (also beyond our control), and internal change that we choose, which is within our control.

The first form of change — external change that is beyond our control — usually breeds the greatest resistance and causes the greatest stress. Technological and cultural changes, shifts in politics and economics, war and natural disasters, and rising rates of crime fall into this category. Because all these things are beyond our control, we feel helpless in the face of them. We complain about the state of the world, and we allow anxiety to govern our thoughts and feelings. This form of change runs over us, leaving us feeling battered and broken.

The second form of change-internal change beyond our control-comprises the normal, natural life transitions that often cause stress and strain and leave us feeling helpless. Aging, death of loved ones, broken relationships, forced change of job, and moving are some examples of the second form of change. Because these life experiences involve other people or forces beyond our control, they are very close to us. We can watch as they occur, all the while feeling powerless to affect them. Once again, the church affords a valuable healing ministry to everyone who is facing this type of change.

The third form of change — internal change within our control — is the easiest to deal with, and it is the form of change most likely to be embraced. Because we choose it, this kind of change is something we anticipate eagerly.

The birth of a child, a new career, going to school, buying a house or a car, or entering a new relationship are all radical changes; but they tend to be very positive. Even though they are things we desire, they still create stress in our lives. All change causes stress, whether it is good change or negative change. However, when the change is positive, and when the benefits of the change are self-evident, it is much easier to adapt.

The key to embracing all forms of change is enabling people to increase their sense of control and understanding so that they might comprehend the benefits that they receive through the change. In one respect, this is a "looking for the silver lining" process. Not every change is good, and sometimes it is nearly impossible to find something to celebrate. But one thing that is always within our control is attitude, and the way we choose to respond to change will make all the difference in the world. Choosing a positive response to change is easier in community than it is individually. In community we find support through the sharing of ideas and experiences that make coping with change more manageable.

At a conference of approximately 240 church secretaries, I asked how many of them began their careers on manual or electric typewriters. About eighty percent responded positively. I then asked how many of them currently worked on word processors or personal computers. The response to the second question was around ninety-eight percent. Next, I asked how many of the people who began on typewriters would like to discard their computers and go back. Not one hand went up. Last, I asked people to share the stories about when they first made the shift from their typewriters to computers. The horror stories were endless. They talked about how much they hated learning the computer, how angry they got, how frustrated, how much they resisted the change. Some told how they wished they could throw the computer out a window or throw the pastor who suggested the change out the window. Virtually no one in the room shared a story of a smooth transition from the old paradigm to the new. And yet, no one wanted to go back. Enough time had passed for the secretaries to gain understanding of the ways they benefited from the change.

Every person, no matter how Christian or unselfish, carries within one unspoken question: "What's in it for me?" When we see the value of an experience or practice, we will gladly engage in it. When value is added to our lives, we look forward to making whatever change is necessary to receive it. Very few people would turn down a sizable gift of money, but more money is a change; and it brings with it stress and anxiety. The nature of change is that it will happen no matter what. Change is value-neutral — it is neither good nor bad. Our response is what gives value to change. If we will embrace change, receiving what change has to teach and give us, we will find the future to be a much more appealing place. If we fight change, the sheer amount of energy it requires will beat us down and eventually break us.

To respond to change in a positive way, it is first important to develop a plan. Change management is a skill that everyone can acquire and that leaders should model and teach. When change — or a need for change — is recognized, it is important to begin to build awareness of what the change is and why it is happening. This leads to a process of creating understanding around the change. The more we understand something, the less we fear it. If external change is happening, we can carefully assess the positives and negatives and begin to respond in the healthiest and most productive way. When the change is internal, we can plot our course to maximize the benefits while minimizing the costs. By taking the time to fully understand the change that is occurring, we increase our receptivity and lessen our stress. We become masters of change, instead of allowing change to master us.

Churches that help people manage change, share information, and build relationships will break free of the inertia that holds them in the old paradigm. Leadership that focuses on these three functions will necessarily be a different kind of leadership for a different kind of church. As leaders, we will need to let go of many of the lesser administrative tasks. Our work will shift from planning and implementing activities to clarifying our identity and creating an environment for growth and faith formation. This shift will propel The United Methodist Church forward into the new faith-forming-community paradigm.

Chapter Eleven Questions

1. Where do people have opportunities to build strong relationships with God and each other in our congregation? How can we improve these opportunities?
2. How clear and transparent are our communication practices? How much of our communication is one-way (monologic)? How much is dialogue or group discussion?
3. How well do we lead and manage change in our church? How well do we help people understand the benefits of change while lessening the negative impact of change (what people feel they are losing or giving up)?
4. How much of our time is spent preparing for the future, and how much is spent managing the present? How might we free more time to look to the future and move from managing today to creating a new tomorrow?

Conclusion

The United Methodist Church is alive and well as it moves forward into the twenty-first century. Despite the immense challenges facing the church of Jesus Christ, it will prevail as it has many times in the past. But just as history repeatedly reveals, the church that emerges on the other side of the paradigm shift will be radically different. We can ill afford to wait for the shift to cease and the dust to settle before deciding what our response will be. Proactive, learning leaders are needed to move us forward. A recentering in the means of grace and a refocusing on our corporate mission are essential. Speaking the language of vision, intuition, feeling, deep desire, and spiritual gifts will become commonplace. Practicing systems thinking, continuous improvement, and change management will prepare us for the transformation that must occur. Breaking the decision-making hierarchies and involving all people in the ministries and programs of the church will usher in a new day of community building and faith formation. People will discover a new level of life exploration as they engage in churches designed to walk with them on a journey of faith, moving with them into relationship with God, others, and the world. The church will break free of the bonds that hold it in the old paradigm, and it will regain its momentum as it moves boldly into the new.

Will that be the end of the story? Of course not. If history teaches us anything, it teaches that as soon as we arrive in the new paradigm, the paradigm again will shift; and we will be challenged once more to become something new. When the next shift occurs, perhaps we will not fight or dread it, but we will welcome the opportunity to change and to grow once more. As we gain a clearer sense of who we are and who God is calling us to be in the twenty-first century, we will hunger to put our knowledge into action. Once more, we will swing from a focus on being to a focus on doing. This is as it should be. Without movement, there is little change. Without change, there is no growth. Without growth, there is only death.

Our church is far from dead. Worldwide, hundreds of thousands of people are coming to know Jesus Christ through the Methodist movement. As we gracefully enter the new paradigm, millions more will hear the good news from us. We are being challenged. We are being called. It is time to take a journey together that will lead us to Jesus Christ by sending us into God's world. It is time to be a new kind of church.

Author's Afterword

A NEW KIND OF CHURCH was originally written in 1998 with my wonderful friend and colleague, Evelyn Burry. It has been an enlightening experience to return to this work to revise and update it. I have been pleasantly surprised by the book — there is some very good stuff here (obviously someone thinks so, to bring it back in print!) — but also find it lacking in a few key areas.

With this unique opportunity to correct some obvious weaknesses I offer the following five additions.

First, pray. Let me say it again. Pray. Pray individually, pray together, pray morning, noon, and night. The only way the church is ever going to realize its full potential is by God's grace and guidance. I know I emphasized the importance of the practice of the means of grace, but I want to be more explicit. Many church leaders I talk with — both laity and clergy — lament that they do not have time to pray. If this is true — if there is no time for prayer — then our priorities are seriously out of whack. I believe it is imperative that we reclaim prayer as the center of our life together as the body of Christ.

We also need to remember that prayer has two parts-what we have to say to God and what God has to say to us. This means we need to make space not only to say our piece to God, but there must be some silence for listening and reflecting. We need to rescue meditation and contemplation from our earlier roots and begin to listen deeply to God's Spirit. This is not wasted time, and it is not of secondary importance to the real work of the church. PRAYER IS THE REAL WORK OF THE CHURCH.

Second, we need to talk to each other. We need to reflect on what we think, feel, hear, believe, hope, dream, worry, wonder, and want in Christian community. We need to spend time together wrestling with the very important question, "What does God want for this church, at this time, and in this place?" As leaders, we need to carve time to study the Scriptures together, to worship together, and to get our hands dirty together in some projects outside the church building. We need to be community to lead community.

Third, we need to give ourselves the time to move to a new reality. I am constantly amazed that congregations that have taken thirty years to get where they are today think they can follow some six week program to get somewhere completely different. The destination isn't the point; the journey is. How we move into God's future is as important as getting there. Remember the Exodus? The trip that should have taken months that took 40 years? That's the one. It's a great model for our transformation into a new kind of church. Don't rush, don't push, don't force, just trust. God will bless all our efforts if we will only step forward in faith.

Fourth, pay attention to the heart. God is already working in the hearts, minds, souls, and spirits of the people. Talk about heart's desires, passions, dreams, and aspirations. Brainstorm, think outside the box, innovate, and for the sake of all that is holy, laugh. The church-of all the places on earth-should be the place where we catch glimpses of the kingdom of God. We focus much too much attention in the church on reasonable, rational, linear processes. We inadvertently kill any spontaneity, enthusiasm, or spirit. (I have some fairly strong opinions on what we should do with *Robert's Rules*, but I'll leave that to your imagination . . .)

Last, we need to know what difference we make. We must stop only counting our inputs — how many people join the church, attend worship, give money, or support our programs — and begin to understand the impact of our outputs — how people are living differently in the world due to their involvement in our congregation. How are people growing in their faith, developing their relationship with God, behaving differently at home, school, office, and in the community? How is the light of Christ evident through each and every one of our participants? How is God's creation better because we exist? These are simple, yet monumental questions.

I am more convinced today than I was a decade ago that The United Methodist Church can be a primary vehicle through which God transforms this world. I am convinced that our congregations can become centers for grace, justice, caring, healing, and deep spiritual intimacy. I believe that today, even more people hunger for meaning, purpose, and connection. Now more than ever, people want a new kind of church.

Appendix

Congregational Core Values Exercise

Core values are the underlying beliefs and principles upon which we base our opinions, decisions, and actions. Evolving from the Latin word, valére (to be of worth, to be strong), values help us understand what is fundamentally important to us and why we do the things we do.

This exercise helps identify and clarify values. It is not intended to make value judgments of right or wrong, good or bad. While each community of faith struggles with which values are appropriate, the focus of this exercise is to bring the existing values of the group to light as a starting point of deeper exploration about how we understand our identity as the church of Jesus Christ. Our understanding of the mission of the church and our particular vision for being the church in the world is determined by the values each person holds.

It is important to keep in mind that values provide the foundation for actions. When people offer "action words" as values, probe deeply to find the underlying beliefs and principles that compel the action by simply asking, "Why?" If someone says "worship" is a value, ask him or her, "But why do we worship?" The desire to be in connection with God to be a better, stronger person is a value that leads us to worship. The best way to clarify the root values underlying our actions is to ask why.

Throughout the exercise, simply record the answers given. For the purposes of this exercise, values are neither positive or negative, good or bad, right or wrong. Values simply are. This exercise is a way of naming the current reality — seeing the current values of the people who are present. Further discussions based on this experience will undoubtedly emerge.

Exercise:

Gather people into groups of no less than three, no more than seven. Define values as "the beliefs and principles upon which we base our opinions, decisions, and actions." Give individuals ninety seconds to list on a sheet of paper the values upon which they think the church should be based. At the conclusion of the ninety seconds, ask the participants to select the one or two most critically important values on their list. Give them thirty seconds to do this. In the small groups, have each person talk about his or her critically important values. Then ask the small groups to select one or two values to be shared with the whole group. Give the groups ten to fifteen minutes for this discussion. As a large group, list all the critical values of each small group. Note the variety, and remind the group that one value is no better than any other — this list reflects the many values that the group deems important. If there are any "action words" in the list, challenge the small groups to think more deeply by asking the "why" questions.

For many people in the group, talking about values will be a new experience. For some, it may produce anxiety, frustration, or anger. People hold their values very dear, and some may not want to justify why they feel the way they do. In fact, some may not know why they feel the way they do. Make this exercise as safe, nonconfrontational, and nonjudgmental as possible. Remind the group that this is an identification exercise, not a prioritization exercise.

Ask each small group to take another fifteen minutes to discuss the implications for the church, based on the created list of values. Does the work of the church truly reflect this list of values? What do these values mean to the mission of "making disciples of Jesus Christ"? How do these values shape the congregation's vision for ministry? How do we strategically plan for the future, building upon the foundation of our core values? At the conclusion of the fifteen minutes, have small groups share insights with the larger group.

Endnotes

1 Sources for this information include: *The New York Public Library Desk Reference*. Third Edition (New York: Macmillan, 1998); *Compton's Interactive Encyclopedia*. Version 5.1.0, 1997 edition. Softkey Multimedia Inc., 1996.

2 Gregory Bateson, *Mind and Nature: A Necessary Unity* (New York: Dutton, 1979).

3 Fred Pratt Green, *When the Church of Jesus* (#592, *United Methodist Hymnal*. Nashville: United Methodist Publishing House, 1989). Words copyright © 1969, Hope Publishing Company, Carol Stream, IL 60188. All rights reserved. Used by permission.

4 Webster's II, New Riverside Dictionary (Berkley Books: New York, 1984).

5 Susan Mitchell, *The Official Guide to American Attitudes*, 1st edition (Ithaca, New York: New Strategist Publications, 1996).

6 Ezra Earl Jones, *Quest for Quality in the Church: A New Paradigm* (Nashville: Discipleship Resources, 1993), p. 19.

7 Margaret Wheatley, *Lessons from the New Workplace*. CRM Films, 1996.

8 Seminars held in 1997 and 1998 by Dan R. Dick, General Board of Discipleship.

9 The term "balcony perspective" is borrowed from Richard Broholm and Douglas Johnson's book about the role of trustees, *A Balcony Perspective*, published by the Robert K. Greenleaf Center in Indianapolis, Indiana, copyright © 1993.